ANTHOLOGY OF POETRY
BY
YOUNG AMERICANS®

2010 EDITION
VOLUME XXV

Published by Anthology of Poetry, Inc.

©*Anthology of Poetry by Young Americans*®
2010 Edition
Volume XXV
All Rights Reserved©

Printed in the United States of America

To submit poems
for consideration in the year 2011 edition of the
Anthology of Poetry by Young Americans®,
go to: www.anthologyofpoetry.com or

      Anthology of Poetry, Inc.
      PO Box 698
      Asheboro, NC 27204-0698

Authors responsible
for originality of poems submitted.

Anthology of Poetry, Inc.
307 East Salisbury • P.O. Box 698
Asheboro, NC 27204-0698

Paperback ISBN: 978-1-883931-79-7
Hardback ISBN: 978-1-883931-78-0

Anthology of Poetry by Young Americans®
is a registered trademark of
Anthology of Poetry, Inc.

How can you expect children to write poetry? They don't know anything about life's experiences, they know very little about how poems should be structured, and their vocabulary is so limited, there is no way they'll be able to express themselves. Oh, really? If that's what you think, you have another think coming! As a matter of fact, just keep reading and hold on to your chair. You're about to be transported to a world where kids *can* write poetry, they *can* express themselves, and they *can* structure poems any way that they'd like. But what about life experience? Well, that's the best part. By describing the world as they see it, limited only by their imagination, that's when we are truly transported; transported to our past, our future, or to another way of looking at our present. Children write poetry? You bet! And it should be required reading for everyone old enough to read.

But kids don't usually just sit down and start writing on their own. Of course they need some training and some motivation, but mostly what they need is a parent or teacher who inspires them and who instills in them a love for creative writing.

We offer our sincere congratulations to all the students whose heartfelt work earned them a place in this publication, and our sincere gratitude to the parents and teachers who inspired them. We are proud to present this 2010 edition of the ***Anthology of Poetry by Young Americans***®. By showcasing these poems we hope that this forum will serve as a permanent form of recognition and as an encouragement to all the young authors who *"can't"* write poetry.

The Editors

Registry of Authors

GRANDMAS

Grandmas are sweet.
They love birds when they tweet.
Grandmas will bake you cookies and cake,
But don't overeat for goodness sake!

Grandmas take you to the Grand,
You hope they have your candy brand.
Then you go home and say, "I had a blast,"
She will say, "Good, but I loved the cast."

When they take you to the store,
They buy you watermelon galore.
And when my grandma says she's broke,
My grandpa begins to cough and choke.

My grandma is the best,
I love her more than all the rest.
Even though we leave her home a mess,
We fill her life with happiness.

Kodi Hettich
Age: 11

MY LIFE AS A RANCHER

I live on a ranch
We move cows quite a bit
We get up pretty early
And then we go to it

We work the cows in a chute
We have to give them vaccine
They won't move so we give them the boot
When that's all done it's time to head home

We move the cows home in the fall
They spend the summer away
Sometimes it can be a long haul
But that's my life as a rancher

Ben Linn

I LOVE MY DOG

I think my dog is funny, I think my dog is cute.
I think my dog is funny because he barks at nothing,
I think my dog is cute because he chases nothing.
I'm pretty sure my dog is funny because he wakes me up,
I'm pretty sure my dog is cute
because he lays in my bed at night.
I know my dog is funny, I know my dog is cute.

Jacob Linn

I LIKE BUDDY

She plays with me.
She will bring me the ball.
I give her food.
She likes it when I give her treats.
I like to play with her.
She is a springer spaniel.
She is my favorite dog I have ever had.
I love her.
We love her.
She is my favorite dog I could ever have.

Austin Kratochvil
Age: 8

THE FUNNY BIRD

A beak more than a foot long,
Long enough to be a bridge.
Scruffy brown feathers
And beady black eyes.

Fast when running,
But cannot fly.
The Funny Bird is his name,
And being a funny bird is his game.

Molly Anderson

DOGS AND PUPPIES

My puppies and dogs lick my face and like to play
They chase the cat around the house sometimes
I trip over the dogs
They play with the cat.

Jordyn Bushy
Age: 6

VOLLEYBALL

I step out on the court and my heart's pounding
It's the other team's turn to serve
The score is 24 to 24
We are tied and need two more points to win
They serve it over
The back row bumps it to me
I set it up high into the air
The spiker gets the kill
We get the point but still need one more
Now it's our turn to serve
It's over and the ball's in play
Serve receive gets it to me
I set it up high again
The spiker gets it and slams it down
It's a kill
We win!!

Emily Linn

MY TWO DOGS

They lived with us
Cute
Friendly
Like to play
Bite softly
One is white
One is brownish-grayish
Run around
My brothers and I chase them
Snowball walks on his back legs
Paulie jumps high
Now they are sad because they are separated

Nate Minello
Age: 8

TOYS

Toys are fun
Toys are a boat and a Game Boy and a Wii Fit
I have more
Like a doll and a ball and a slide
I like a lot of toys
Toys are my favorite
I like kites too
I love my toys

Jaden Elizabeth Rose
Age: 7

BALL

B alls are fun
A lways a blast
L augh a lot
L ove playing with them.

Kaleb Lux
Age: 11

REED

R for radical
E for energetic
E for everlasting
D for done with this poem

C. Reed Minello
Age: 10

H elpful
E nergetic
A dorable
T ruthful
H appy
E ntertaining
R unner

Heather Okeson
Age: 6

RENEW

R ecycle
E verything
N ow and always to
E nhance our
W orld.

Dawson Hertz
Age: 10

AROUND THE TRACK

The black horse is very fast
He's never come in last
There he goes around the track
He's way ahead of the pack

The others are way behind
They must be in a bind
We're almost done
But we're having lots of fun

My horse loves to run
We always have lots of fun
Across the finish line we go
His hooves just seem to flow

We got first of course
Because I have an awesome horse.
We won the whole entire thing
I'll try again in the spring.

Stephanie Klatt
Age: 12

THE TRUE CANCER

Would you love me more if I was dying?
It's a concept I often speculate.
Yes with pain and tears in my eyes.
If I had moments left of life
   would you do everything you could?
Maybe, but also everything you should?
Perhaps you would accept everything I really am.
Not how you think I should be.

I know you would be more proud.
I know that you would finally realize.
But don't you know that I could leave today?
Or maybe tomorrow.
If you could comprehend, it would be different.
You would love me more.
You would take joy in my happiness.
Sadness in my sorrows.
Life in my living.

Because you don't know when I will go,
   you treat me the same.
But I know if I only had months, weeks, days,
   or moments . . .
Oh, the change!
How you think of me.
The shame that you left a sting.
You will have more tears than my tears.

Realize that we are all dying.
Fading on our own life cycle.
We don't know how long we have.
We can't be sure when.
Be pleased with me as I am.

Kelse Hanson
Age: 16

CANDY

Candy is so sweet
It's so good to eat
Hershey's is my favorite candy
It is very dandy

I don't want to share it
Because I will throw a fit
You can have my Skittles I don't care
As long as you don't stare

Sometimes you can have my Snickers
Only if you don't try to bicker
I really don't like Kisses but I eat them anyway
You can have my Kisses on Sunday

Hot Tamales I hate the most
They make my tongue roast
Candy I love a lot
Broccoli I do not

Jared Phelps
Age: 11

THE M POEM

M was a magic man.
He looks in magazines.
He also likes to munch on muffins.
He made a machine one day.
He never gets mad.
He can make many magnificent cakes.
He is a master.
He reads maps.
He loves meals.
He doesn't like mud.

Matthew Hennessy
Age: 8

BORED

Bored to me is the colors of ebony and ivory
like in an old movie.
Bored tastes like cake without frosting.
It smells like bland, barbecue sauce.
When you're bored,
people's voices sound like bla, bla, bla, bla.
Bored feels like a brisk, frigid, rainy day.
It looks like a snoring, drooling, old, hound dog.

Haley J. Gullickson
Age: 11

REVENGE

Revenge is flaming red.
It's delicious yet bitter as Lemonheads.
It's spicy chili on a hot afternoon.
A red demon laughing inside my head.
A feeling as a tingling feeling inside me
like a monkey ready to jump out.
Revenge is flaming red, an inferno.

Revenge is a delight to have,
but it gets you into a lot of trouble
when you don't be careful
so be cautious.

Michael Hatzenbuhler
Age: 11

RELAXED

Relaxed is the romantic red and sweet orange sunset
slowly vanishing.
I can taste the chunky peanut butter in my mouth
and the smell of fresh bread baking.

I can hear the soft yet massaging music.
It feels like I am lying on a soft fluffy cloud
or in a nice warm bubble bath.
I can now see a faint candlelight around me.

Jessica T. George
Age: 11

SIX LITTLE KITTENS

Six little kittens playing in the barn
Guess what? They are not playing with yarn.
Their mother takes them back to the yard.
Uh-oh there's a dog on guard!

Under the van six kittens dive.
Oh but wait there's only five!
Oh no we're missing one!
There he is playing in the sun.

The dog is sniffing all about.
Look out! The kittens shout.
The little kitten comes running back.
Because the dog was looking for a snack.

The dog is sniffing around the car.
Then he shouts there the kittens are!
The kittens think this could be the end.
But the dog just wanted to be their friend.

So the dog and the kittens fell asleep,
And none of them made even a peep.
The dog and the kittens became friends,
So here it is our story ends.

Tucker Johnson
Age: 12

VIKINGS

Adrian Peterson, my favorite player,
Is the best in the game
He's gonna make it to the Hall of Fame
When Adrian scores
The crowd roars

The Vikings defense is great too
With a sack the sound in the crowd grew
Brett Favre can throw the ball
You can find Percy Harvin's jersey in the mall

Their offensive line
Is really fine
Their blocking skills
Gives me chills

When they throw it deep
I don't make a peep
When they run the ball
I hear a call

Brandon Jenkins
Age: 11

THE BUG

I am a small, small bug
With a small, small rug.
I have a flower
That is a coward
But it loves to hug!

Abbey Bruno

BASKETBALL

The game started
The other player darted
For the ball
He hit the wall

I shot a three
The crowd went "wee"
The other team shot a two
The crowd went "boo"

I shot a three and swish
The crowd made a wish
I stole the ball
The ref gave me a call

I tripped someone
We had a lot of fun
I shot the ball
We won it all

Tonya Dickson
Age: 11

ROSEY

Rosey, my kitty, ran away.
Mama left the door open.
I feel sad.

Grace Andrea Dahl
Age: 5

THE DOCTOR'S OFFICE

When I go to the doctor's office
It makes me feel really nauseous
The big needles they jab in my vein
Give me very great pain!

When they check my reflexes
I wish I could be in Texas
At the end of the checkup
I'll go eat hot dogs with ketchup

Feeling no more pain
Gives me a smarter brain
Being really brave
Makes me feel good not to be in a cave

When I go home I'll play in the rain
Or maybe even test my brain
I'm so glad to be out of there
It made me want to pull my hair

Layton Birdsell
Age: 11

TAKE ME OUT TO THE POOL SIDE

Take me out to the pool side,
take me out for the slides.
Bring some pretzels and peanut butter
I don't care if I ever get dry.
For it's splash, splash, splash
for the swimmers.
If I can't swim anymore
it's a shame.
For it's dive, splash,
swim and go
on slides.
In the
swimming
pool.

Giselle Rintoul
Age: 10

IF I HAD . . .

If I had the legs of a cheetah,
I would run fast.
I would catch my food fast.
I'd protect my cubs.
But I wouldn't walk slow,
Because turtles do that.

Hannah Candrian
Age: 10

16

A SECOND CHANCE

You can use a rifle for coyote season.
A 22-250 will make you stay another day.
Hunting with friends is so much fun.
It's not the kill but the companionship is the reason.

Being outside is so much fun.
Searching for coyotes
And driving the countryside
Waiting to use my gun.

We spot a coyote and jump out.
We load the gun and aim to shoot.
We change our minds when pups appear.
The mother must live without a doubt!

The coyote family disappeared out of sight.
I was glad to give the mother a second chance!
The pups will be happy and not so sad.
I know what I did was right!

Kaylee Anne Knutson
Age: 11

FAMILY

My mom cares for Adam
Together they're in love
Adam cares for my mom
Their relationship soars like a dove

I love my sister
Though sometimes we fight
I know she loves me too
Even though sometimes she says go fly a kite

Our family is together
We love each other so
We can do so much more now
This family can only grow

My sis and I love Adam
He cares for us so much
He is very fun
He has a special touch

Alexus Eve Mahlum
Age: 10

TREES

They always start small
then they begin to grow tall
high into the sky

Kaylen Barstad
Age: 12

IF I HAD THREE WISHES
I WOULD WISH FOR . . .

I wish I was taller,
I wish I could see my grandmas
and grandpas more often,
I wish my sister
wouldn't bite me on my knee
when she gets mad at me.

Michaela Hixson
Age: 10

Insects
black and yellow
head, thorax, abdomen
They have stingers
Queen hornet

Hannah Keller
Age: 9

We walked in a cave
It was dark and had black bats
Clinging to the wall

Tayler Hoyt
Age: 11

BLUE JAY

Blue jay soaring by
Its glistening wings swishing
Gliding near the pond

Kiana Shui
Age: 11

WINTER

I always like winter best.
You can eat cookies fresh from the oven
And dark chocolate brownies,
While you drink delicious warm apple cider;
Listen to the motor of the ski lift;
Go outside and wrestle with my dog;
Or stay inside and play with my hamsters;
Fred, Biney, and Pip Squeek.
I always like winter best!

Lexi Jordheim

Filled with fluffy clouds
I am a powdery blue
Floating in the air

Noah Haagenson

NIGHT

The stars at night shine
The air, very cool and crisp
No sounds are made now.

Raine Bertelsen
Age: 11

FEAR

Fear is like a pitch-black room.
It tastes like a dead plum.
It reeks like a rotten cow.
It sounds like people taunting you
in a high-pitched voice.
My heart feels like it is pounding fifty miles per hour.
Fear looks like a shriveled-up sorcerer in my room.

Evan J. Gullickson
Age: 11

The teal blue water
Shown through the ice from sunlight
Peaceful blue water

Alexa Engelbrecht
Age: 12

AN ELF WHO BOUGHT A NEW SHELF

There once was an elf,
Who bought a new shelf,
He found a bug,
He squished it with a mug,
And found a boy named Ralph.

Caden Schatz

HAPPY MY HORSE

My horse is really fast,
He is really nice.
Appaloosa is his breed
He likes to run free.
My friends gave him to me.
Jumping over puddles
It is his way of having fun

Kassandra Linn

Smoky
skinny, funny
running, hiding eating
Smoky is really cute!
Fluffy

Dylan Schock
Age: 10

THE SOUND OF A TRAIN

Beautiful train
Hear your whistle
Through the air
The sound of your whistle
Is so beautiful
Your whistle is so loud
Your horn says
Get out of the way cars
You blow your horn
When you take off
You blow your horn
And say
All aboard

Garrett Smith
Age: 10

BLUE IS A SAD DAY

Blue is sad
Blue is a berry
Blue day is sad
Blue you can't stand
Blue isn't fun
Blue is horrible
Blue is a light color
Blue is fun sometimes
Blue is great
Blue is a great color
Blue is really fun
Blue you can play with

Jonathan Stanford
Age: 9

BLUE

Blue is the color of my room,
And that is true.
Blue is the sky on a nice
Summer day.
Blue is a dove
That many people love.
Blue reminds me of fresh laundry.
Blue is the color of sadness.

Haylee Linstad

RED

The leaves are turning red
By the time you get in your bed
You get up early that morning
See your mom
Making bread
Later that night
You start a bonfire
See the red flames
Light up the night
Then you climb into your warm beds
Shut off the light
The next morning you get dressed
Go sled on your brand-new red sled
Then you go inside
Crawl into your red bed.

Branson Frost
Age: 9

BLUE IS A GREAT COLOR

Blue is like the color of the sky
Blue is the smell of a blueberry pie
Blue is like the dark ocean
Blue is my favorite color

Olivia Bechtold
Age: 9

PINK

Pink is like a flower
My tongue is pink
My nose is pink
My palm is pink
There is nail polish that is pink
Water bottles can be pink
And so can flamingos

Teghan Vermandel
Age: 11

THE COLOR OF BLUE

Blue is the beautiful sky
Blue is a color in the rainbow
Blue is the color of the ocean
Blue is the color of your eyes
Blue is the color of your dress
Blue is the color of your flower
Blue is the color of a dolphin
Blue is the color of your book cover
Blue is the color of your chair
Blue is the color of your coat
Blue is the color of your hair
Blue is the color of your shirt
Blue is the color of your room

Hannah Petrie
Age: 9

PINK

Pink is like a rainbow
In the sky
Pink is like pictures on a wall
And paintings in a box
Pink is like a ribbon in the sky
And in the sun
Pink is like a flamingo
Standing still
In the sun and sky

Michelle Wipf
Age: 10

THE SOUNDS OF A TRAIN

I hear the wheels on the tracks
Roaring
They run towards me saying
Toot, Toot
My heart is beating
The passengers are hollering with excitement
The engineer is hollering
It is time to get off
The engineer is calling
All aboard
And it goes off into the sunset

Kaitlyn Ohmstede
Age: 9

WHEN THE TRAIN COMES BY

When the train comes by
They honk the horn loud
You hear the people shouting, it's noisy!
You can hear the babies crying and whining
You see the people opening the window
And shouting hi everyone
Nobody really likes it when the train comes by

Tyler Seboldt
Age: 9

THE RIVER

Silent and calm
Liquid clear
A warm feeling in cold air
It looks like glass
But if you step in you'll sink
Sink into the frigid spring snow melt
I sit there on the rock ledge
Not far from that liquid ice
You say you cannot see me
But I'm there
I am the voice that whispers these crisp words
You say I'm the wind but I am the storyteller

Callie Wollenburg
Age: 12

BEWILDERED

Bewildered is a rosy pink,
Somewhat like an unripened apple,
In both flavor and sound,
(for when an apple drops
it hardly makes a sound,
and is not very easily found)
Feels like strolling through a graveyard,
Looks like the specter you find there,
Yet is a slicing blade,
And a tolling bell.

Vaida R. Crofutt
Age: 11

KITTENS

They are small.
Kittens are fun.
They have little paws.
They are cute.
Kittens have little faces.
They usually have green or blue eyes.
They meow.
Kittens run.
They are fun.
I love kittens.

Wyatt Knoke

PRO SKIER

The day of extreme skiing has begun
One competitor is John Smitee
And the other is Michael Dunn
First Michael Dunn will ski

Through the deep snow he skis
Hoping his time will be fair
Weaving through the tight spruce trees
Getting face shots here and there

The finish line is getting near
Michael Dunn's time will be great,
    if his run does not end in fate
Michael Dunn is finished, now he holds up his gear
Michael Dunn is happy he didn't finish late

Now it is John Smitee's run to ski
He wants to ski very fast
Hoping he will not blow out a knee
John Smitee does not want to finish last

He skis through the deep snow
Off cliffs and through trees
John Smitee is putting on quite a show
He is great at controlling his skies

John Smitee sees the finish line coming up
Only one cliff left to jump
John Smitee does not see the jump; all he sees is a lump
He loses a ski and lands on his back
    with a quiet "wump"

John Smitee loses the race to Michael Dunn
John Smitee is very depressed
Michael Dunn goes home to have fun
John Smitee goes home to rest

John Smitee hopes to defeat Michael Dunn
In the race next year
Dunn hopes his winning streak is not done
Every day the race is getting nearer and nearer

Logan Beck

TOOT TOOT

I hear the train's horn
It goes Toot Toot
People hear the train
They are standing in the rain
The train goes by
And splashes people with water
A lot of people wish it were hotter
Some like the sound
Others like the background
We will hear the horn go . . .
Toot Toot
Chuga, Chuga, Chugh, Chuga
Toot Toot

Metayah Caster
Age: 9

IF YOU LOVED ME

If you loved me, you'd be there for me
To help me do the things I want to do.
My whole life wouldn't be only for you,
Nor would my love determine who you'd be.

I want you to respect what I do well,
To share the joy I feel when I succeed,
To give me the encouragement I need,
To be my wings, not my protective shell.

I love you, and I want you to be mine,
But I would never say you're not allowed
To be a person who would make me proud,
To step outside into your own sunshine.

RyAnn Rath

THE WIND

Whipping dust onto my face and into my eyes.
Snatching papers from grasping hands,
And spreading seeds to grow new life.
Rounding up an angry storm—
Thrashing about as if having a seizure
Leaves tickling my face . . .

Hannah Wollenburg
Age: 14

TAFFY

T errific
A nimal
F un
F urry
Y ou will love him!

Alexandria Murphy

FIND A WAY

My friends are far away from here,
But I won't shed a single tear.
For I will see them again someday,
Somehow I must find a way.

A way back home where I belong,
I hope and pray it won't take long.
While I've been wandering and lost,
All my friends it might have cost.

All this time that I've been away,
People have needed me every day.
As I walked away I felt their stare,
But back then I just didn't care.

I left them there, all alone in fear,
But they never shed one single tear.
For they knew I'd be back someday
They had faith that I'd find a way.

Bridget Gustad

WINTER

Wind and snow
Wind blows the snow
Fast and cold
Very fast and very cold

Cold and bold
The wind is cold
The wind is bold
The wind is shockingly cold

The wind is shockingly bold
Fast as it passed
Snow blows fast
Very fast when it passed

Long and song
Wind is long
The wind is like a song
It is a very long song

White and light
The snow is white
The snow is light
The snow is white and sometimes light

Hold and told
The snow will hold
Just as people have told
Snow is going to hold; well that's what people have told

May and away
The snow may
It might go away
The snow may go away

Done and sun
The snow is done
Here comes the sun
Now here is the sun and the snow is done

Juliann Kenaston
Age: 13

WHISPERS

Whispers or voices in my head?
I am not able to tell.
A raspy voice in my ear?
I hide with great great fear.
I seem to be shrinking with the more I fear.
Are the voices getting near?
I am hiding with much more fear.
What's this I hear I should not cower in fear?
As the whispers creep near.
I'm sure I'm not insane.
Or am I just saying this in vain.
I wake up just a dream I say.
When suddenly I hear a whisper.
Don't cower in fear.

Taylor Hallman

PROMISE

I promise to love you,
No matter what you do.
I'll be there,
Always to care.
I will love you 'til the day I die,
Because I'll never say good-bye.
When you are near, my heart skips a beat,
Because you make me complete.
When we are apart,
It breaks my heart,
I will love you,
That's a promise I'll do!

Carolee Crocker

WAITING

I'll be here for you always in a day.
Waiting, waiting just so we can go play.
You don't show on the playground, why not?
Did you have to go somewhere?
Now we can't play with the jump rope I bought.
Oh well it's your fault.
I'm like this I waited and waited for you to come,
But you left me standing here cold, faded, and numb.

Opal Hill

THE DAY

The day will come
When I will leave
Please don't cry
Try to smile
I'm not dying
I will return
Please don't think
That you are losing your baby
I really will miss you
I will come home a lot more than you think
Please stay my mother
And love me all the same
For I won't be gone
For as long as it seems
Please come see me
When you get the chance
My future is calling
So let me go
Please I will return
On the day
Love your baby girl

Frankee Bice

VOICE OF A GHOST

So peculiar she was,
How she grew a field of hope
From nothing at all.
Her good luck wish sent
On the wings of a butterfly,
Crumbled to dust.
Worthless words.
Rain, steam, and smoke
Dance around each other
Moving forward in an uneasy dream.
She discovered a hidden piece of her heart.
Pointless words.
Peach-blossom lips and porcelain skin
Clear eyes with an empty soul,
No tears left, no more feeling.
The girl's shadow grew thinner and thinner
So much pain, so numb.
Words lost in time,
She is the voice of a ghost.
No more words.

Sierra Dawn Speer
Age: 16

THE TRAIN STATION

Hear people shouting
Move move
Coming through
Hearing whistles blow
Choo Choo
Conductors shouting
All aboard
Workers shouting
Stop
Officers arresting people

Bailey Chaffin
Age: 9

SILENCE

The snow falling, no howling wolves,
no rustling trees.

Silence. The dark house, cat slinking,
children sleeping.

Silence. Pencils writing, children thinking,
brains working.

Isaac Fisher
Age: 9

THE GIRL WITH NO NAME

Sometimes a person is born differently
They may not do everything
As everyone else would
There is a person like that now
That person is
The girl with no name
She wakes up in the morning
And goes to her boring destination
When she arrives she sulks through the day
Her life is routine
And she knows it
That girl with no name
She never utters a word
Sits silently alone
Nobody knows what she's thinking
Maybe she really has no friends
But nobody knows a thing about
The girl with no name
Although she may not know it
She's more popular than she thinks
Every time she passes by
People notice
And they whisper gossip about
The girl with no name
She doesn't care
Their words don't hurt her
She's perfectly happy
No fights with friends
And no one to bother her
Whenever she feels like being alone

The girl with no name
At times though
She doesn't think that this is so great
She keeps to herself
Nobody knows who she really is
She truly is the girl with no name
The next day she walked up to
A very random somebody
She extended a hand and gave a name
And people actually listened
It was the biggest surprise
For the girl with a new name

Marissa Sederlin
Age: 13

THE WHITE TIGER

Its eyes flickered,
Its tail swayed,
It slowly made its way to its prey,
Hunger filled its eyes,
The white fur on her brushed against a leaf,
Her teeth turned to a grin,
She leaped forward but missed,
Again she tried but missed angrily,
As her prey ran away she snarled in regret,
She will find something else,
Maybe something tastier,
She bounded off to find her prey.

Kassey Denker
Age: 11

DANCING

Dancing is something I really enjoy!
It's better than playing with a toy.

I jump and jump and point my feet!
I twirl around and work up heat!

Then I go home and rest,
After doing my very BEST!!!

Lauren Alt
Age: 7

THE LEGION

Cling, Clang, Smash,
The metal bashes together,
I see them coming up the hill,
Like a sea of red, or a sea of blood,
I see them as death nears me,
There is no stopping them,
Here come their javelins,
They block out the sun,
Then the shining glint of metal comes,
Stab, slash, thrust,
I drop slowly to the ground,
Then I feel the fear and terror,
The fear and terror that the legion has brought.

Nicholas Smerker
Age: 13

LET'S SMILE

It's better to smile,
And not to frown!
A frown will only pull people down!

A smile makes everyone upbeat!
And I think that would be neat!

Both are contagious, so make your choice!
It's better to smile, rejoice, rejoice!!

Rianna O'Connell
Age: 9

CHICO

Chico is my dog,
But I want a frog.

Chico is furry and fat,
But I want a bat!

Chico likes to bark,
But I want a shark!!

Chico is white and black,
But I want my cat back!

Beretta Flink
Age: 7

TWO CATS

I had two cats,
But one ran away.
I hope he will come back someday!

Now I have one
To play with after school!
I pet and cuddle him—Oh, what fun!
I think he's really cool!

Cameron LaFond
Age: 7

INTEGRITY

Have you ever told someone around you a lie?
Do you feel the guilt inside?
Do you feel it scream and cry?
When you have a consequential decision to make,
Do you pick the decision you were told not to take?
Do you hear that voice in your mind?
Does it ask you "who will this hurt?"
And what real happiness will I find?
Can I mend the choices I've made?
If you've asked yourself these questions,
You are trying, and soon the guilt will slowly fade,
But next time will you avoid such foolish deeds?
Will you have integrity?
Will you be truthful and ignore your selfish needs?

Lauren Coon

WINTRY NIGHTS

The trees are very still,
The birds are very ill.
It is a cold wintry night,
And the moon is very bright.
The stars in the sky,
Reflect off of my eye.
The snow falls on the ground,
As I hear a howling sound,
As I look out my window
I see speckles of snow,
Yet a light shadow of a fox,
I try to show my brother as he talks.
He does not realize the wonders of a snowy winter night,
When the moon is not bright.

Alexis Ryder
Age: 11

SOCCER

Black and white spots, and, oh, so round!
This is the ball I use to score.
I kick it hard, it hits the ground!!
I want to score more and more.

Rylee Johnson
Age: 8

MY ROOM

My room is such a mess,
It causes me so much stress.
Clothes everywhere,
It's a big nightmare.

Pizza two years old,
Filled with a ton of mold.
Little bugs here and there,
Go in there if you dare.

My mom went in she wasn't afraid,
She came out with an apple halfway decayed.
She said it smelt so bad,
It smelt like the feet of my dad.

Because of the mess we couldn't open the door,
So we had to drill until it was no more.
When you step inside you lose your breath,
You know you're coming to your death.

I couldn't go near because it really smelt,
It almost made my clothes melt.
So I'd advise you to stay away,
Because you'll never get up from where you lay.

Rachel Tuininga
Age: 12

MY DOG, SALLY

My dog, Sally, is quite a dog,
As some would like to say.
With her pointy ears and curly tail,
And thirty pounds she barely weighs.
My dog, Sally, is afraid of cats
One scratched her nose so hard.
Now she shies away from kittens,
No matter how nice they are.
My dog, Sally, hates the snow.
She runs and sits on top of our pump house.
Then she bites my mittens,
Because they are her greatest foe.
My dog, Sally, is a reindeer in the winter months.
She wears felt antlers on her head.
She doesn't seem to mind,
But she looks like a silly dunce.
My dog, Sally is really getting old.
Her fur is growing grey.
Easily she gets cold.
But I love my Sally in every single way.
Everyone loves my dog, who calls to the name of Sal.
They all pet and rub her belly.
But I love Sally most of all,
Because she is my greatest pal.

Danni Jo Bechtold
Age: 11

CHANGE

Change can be good or bad,
depending on what you believe.
Change can be good,
as in a new tradition on Christmas Eve.
Change can be bad,
like a death in the family.
Change can make you cry,
happy, or sad tears.
Change is something that makes a difference,
which is why you can be upset about a thing
and laugh about it later.
Change makes a difference in everyone's life,
no matter if it happens once or twice.
Change can make you sad or happy, laugh or cry,
it can even make you sigh.
Change affects us all,
even if you don't want it to.
Change isn't something
you have the choice to go through,
it is just something you have to go through.

Jade LaDeaux
Age: 12

PIANO RECITAL

I wait nervously,
They call my name
I sit down and take a deep breath
I start to play

As my nervousness goes away,
A smile goes across my face
I pour my heart out with the beautiful music
I play flawlessly and smoothly
The song is "Fur Elise"

I go onto my next song,
It is quick and loud
It sounds like a battle
The song is "1812 Overture"

Then I play the next song,
It's fun, hip, and fast
It makes me feel happy
The song is "Splish Splash"

I stand up,
I am done
The crowd cheers
I walk away with a sigh of relief
At the end of my recital

Lily Huenink
Age: 11

I AM

I am a curious, thankful grandson.
I wonder what exciting exploits I will experience.
I hear my grandma's voice in the back of my head
right before I do something I'll regret.
I see bright, shiny fireworks
when I see the ecstatic faces that my grandparents have
after they observe my report card.
I want to someday be a successful somebody
in the world.
I am a curious, thankful grandson.

I pretend that I know the answer to any question
I feel trapped between questions I can't answer.
I touch my high school diploma
every time I receive a good grade.
I worry that not knowing everything
will embarrass me someday.
I cry when I see a minus behind an A.
I am a curious, thankful grandson.

I understand that someone must know more than me.
I say "I don't understand everything that I know."
I dream that someday the world can live life to its fullest.
I try to live my life to its fullest.
I hope that my grandparents can live long enough
to see my future accomplishments.
I am a curious, thankful grandson.

Lucas Gruwell
Age: 13

ORIGIN

I come from a warm embrace,
A mother's touch,
On a teary face.

I come from a father's glare,
A woeful glance,
So stern, so bare.

I come from a winter's night,
Snow so fresh,
It's blinding white.

I come from a friendly pact,
A sharpened stick,
And a daring act.

I come from a deeper crowd,
A four-string bass,
With volume loud.

I come from my music's strife.
Good or bad,
It is my life.

Zachary A. Leach
Age: 16

SHADES OF BLUE

Light blue like the
Sky after early dawn,
Like the significant tint
Of my diamond tattoo,
Important and deep like
My mother's crystal eyes,
I keep my life classy
And happy and true.

Cobalt blue like the color of the
Most meaningful time of day,
Like the dishes I inherited
From my grandma,
Dark, painful like our car that
Ripped the skin off my thumb,
I spend time alone and
Think of my experiences.

Dark blue like an
Afternoon thunderstorm,
Like my old leg-less couch
Covered in dirt and memories,
Worn and faded like my
Favorite pair of jeans,
I've dealt with a lot, not doing
Well to control myself.

Cyan blue like my
Childhood bathing suit,
Like the sky at 2 p.m.
Out on our boat,
Clear and soothing like the
Water I love jumping into,
My loved ones surround
Me in a cool embrace.

Cerulean blue like a
High-fashion statement,
Like my toenails on
A fall morning,
Stylish and sweet like a
Juicy-Couture-adorned 'tween,
I step and strut and I'm
Proud to act like me.

Kathryn E. Teeghman
Age: 18

As the soft wind blows
Everything will be at peace
It makes me shiver

Olivia Michalik
Age: 11

NATURE

The wind whispers in my ear.
The trees bend low to hear.
The sea sings a song.
The crickets play along.
Nature has a pattern if you pay attention.

The wind whips through my hair.
The sea moistens the air.
The crickets lull you to sleep.
The trees guard your keep.
Nature has jobs that need appreciation.

Joshua Tuininga

THE GRAVEYARD

One gloomy night,
in fact the night before Halloween.
There was a loud creepy sound arising from
the graveyard along the street.
The moon stood there so crisp and bright
not bothered by this haunting night.
Then I thought to myself should I recruit
this sound or remain in bed.
And not take on this night of the living
DEAD . . .

Shannon M. Diviak
Age: 13

54

I was as snug as a bug in my bed on Christmas Eve night
when all of a sudden there came a great fright.
Up on the roof was a hullabaloo
when out of nowhere, I knew what to do.
I tiptoed out of my door
and onto the hallway floor.
I dashed to the stairway, as quiet as a mouse,
making sure not to wake my mom and her spouse.
I went down my stairs in a rush
to see a man who looked mighty flushed.
He looks like a man I know
who goes "Ho, ho, ho!"
He stuffed my stocking with love and care.
I hope I didn't get underwear.
He stood under the chimney and rubbed his big nose.
Soon he went up, up, up, and arose.
I soon went through my head
that I should go back to bed.

Taylor Wilson
Age: 12

Players on the field
Adrenaline rushing in
Yells of the whole crowd

Bryan Padilla
Age: 12

LANCE FROM FRANCE

My neighbor, his name is Lance.
He came here straight from France.
When he sees bees,
He yells help me please,
And does a funny little dance.

Jillian Kozlowski
Age: 9

FISHING

Before I go fishing I get some bait
I don't have to dress up because it's not a date
I put on my messy clothes
And my sandals that show my toes
When I get to the river I toss my line in
Hoping that I will catch one then
At the blink of an eye
I didn't even have to try I got a fish
It was my only wish
We cooked it that night
I went to bed thinking what a fight

Rex Luhman

As I lay in bed asleep I thought I heard
a floorboard creak
I sat up to ponder, and started to wonder,
should I be scared, when barely aware,
of what might lurk down the stairs?
I heard a voice and made a choice,
to stay in bed and await the dread;
that could be around the corner, as I shivered in horror.
To my dismay I heard the voice say,
"Do I dare to give you a scare?
Here I come, don't you fret;
but you'll regret . . . if you stay."
Closer the voice did come,
climbing each step; one by one.
I began to panic, and tried to think quick
of a way to escape this nasty trick.
I heard the hinge squeak and
looked over the cover to peek;
and to my alarm, my fear did come
a sliver of light, which shone so bright
'twas all I could see, through the dark of the night.
The creature walked in, and I cringed at the sight
for what had walked in,
my nerves had not been
ready for the fright, the terror of the night.

Yasmin Mitchel
Age: 13

THE GREATEST WISH

If I had my own genie
Here is what I'd wish for:

I'd wish for world peace,
And maybe get some sleep at night

I'd wish for no more hunger
To help the kids who starve

My mind would clear
And my fears be gone with

As I lay in my bed
I'd think of more wishes

I'd wish for a cure for all cancers
And then spread it around the world

Our lives would be better
And filled with less sadness

I end this poem with one last wish,
I'd wish for all hatred to vanish

So people could fall in love
With the thing that matters most:
Life

Laila Mitchel
Age: 12

AS TIME FLIES!

Flowers blossom, flowers bloom
Butterflies come out of their cocoons
Hibernation ends, children are at play,
We're waiting for another warm day

It's getting warmer, bugs are out
Batter up! Let's scream and shout
People are mowing, fireflies are glowing,
Shining their bright lights about

Falling leaves, dying trees,
Pumpkins are out for Hallow's Eve
School has now started, the bugs have darted
It's getting cold now you can see

Snow is falling, Santa's calling,
Presents are here, we've been waiting all year,
We put up the tree, what a beautiful sight to see
And now the New Year is here

Eric Hoffman
Age: 11

WHEN THE DAY AND NIGHT COLLIDE

After the sun disappears,
the moon reveals itself with the stars that light
up the sky.
The Milky Way streams in a repeating pattern
that moves every second.
Then asteroids sprint across outer space,
crumbling recklessly.
It all happens at night.
When the night fades into morning,
the sun yawns and a new day begins.

Abigail Austin
Age: 11

LONG VOYAGE

My clothes feel very wet,
I feel seasick and dizzy,
It's hard to walk on my two feet,
After the sickness fades away
I run to the crow's nest,
The wind flowing through my hair,
I watch the sunset going down,
After the sun set the full moon came,
My mom and I set up the candles so it was easy to see,
"Land ho" we're here in the New World
We're here.

Meredith Greene
Age: 10

NIGHT

Stars twinkle in a glistening moonlit sky,
The colors of the Milky Way
will shimmer in the starry night.
The moon shines like a blazing prairie fire
in a bird's-eye view,
Shooting stars fill the sky
to make our wishes come true.

Hallie Calhan
Age: 10

SPRING

Spring, spring, spring so happily,
Flowers blooming everywhere.
Tulips growing here and there.
Sunflower seeds spreading everywhere.
Children cheering as loud as can be.
Butterflies fluttering everywhere, that's the key.
Spring is really here as you can see.

On this day there will be buzzing bees.
Buzzing all around the trees.
Baby birds will be chirping lullabies from their nest.
Night by night you're getting rest.
In the morning the hot sun comes blazing in
with its zest.
I like spring, it's the BEST!

Jenny Lundquist

JUST ANOTHER AUTUMN LEAF

The glowing orange sun dipped below the horizon,
Its silky, spider-spun rays withdrawing from sight
The bright purple and pink clouds swiftly glided away,
Stealing the last of the sunset's light

The breathtaking beauty had finally dissolved
As the toasty warmth disappeared from the air
The bountiful leaves vigorously shook on the trees
As if they were taking the hint of despair

Darkness suddenly swept across the sky
Blanketing all the remaining light
Black swallowed all of the leftover colors
The beautiful evening had turned into night

The piercing wind howled violently at the trees
The leaves, in return, only shivered in fright
But the wind would not let go and continued its tantrum
Finally, the leaves leapt up from their branches
And responded in flight

Masses of red, yellow, and orange
Danced around in circles
Colors bursting from the leaves
As it soared through the sky
The wind whipped the leaves in every direction
When right then, just another autumn leaf flew by

The leaf was engulfed in a vibrant shade of red
And as the wind calmed down, it began to gently sway
Everything seemed pleasant as a slight drizzle fell
When suddenly, the edges of the leaf began to fray

Specks of brown dotted the once-flawless red,
Covering every bit of its elegant gown,
Clawing through the bright color full of life,
The young, red leaf had become old and brown

The leaf fluttered helplessly in the wind,
The current forcefully pushing it in the air,
Its gusts lashing out like a whip through the center
The leaf began to crumble apart and tear

As the rain steadily increased its downpour
The wind stopped its whistling without a sound
The wet, soggy leaf that now lay in ruins
Slowly made its way to the ground

The aged leaf, unable to carry on any further,
Decided his resting place would be in the soil
As he settled himself inside of the dirt
He realized that every other autumn leaf
Would face the same turmoil

And little did he realize he was right
When just another autumn leaf flew by.

Anita Venkataswamy
Age: 13

NOVEMBER LEAVES

Yet I see the leaves
An extraordinary weave
Falling through the trees

Jonathan Meehan
Age: 11

HORRIFIED

Horrified is terror,
Hair sticking up, ratty and matted
Eyes bulging out like a paddle ball
Heart pounding out of her chest
The picture of dread

Horrified is frightening
Hands sweaty, palms dripping wet
Teeth chattering like a ticking clock
The image of fear

Horrified is repulsive
Nails are bit until they hurt
Stomach turning like a Ferris wheel
Butterflies won't stop
The painting of anxiety

Morgan Burns
Age: 12

HOT COCOA

Hot cocoa so warm
On a cold winter evening
By the fireplace

Amy Haderspeck
Age: 11

TOGETHER WE UNITE!

U and I were united together when a terrible thing
  happened to America.
N ever forget the time when New York got attacked
  and the life of innocents that never did anything
  wrong and their life is gone.
I t's time to remember the time when our life was
  changed forever from the horrible attack.
T he day looked different because of the smoke. The
  faces looked different because of how the city looked.
E veryone was worried, confused,
  and probably as well furious.
D o you know exactly what I'm talking about? Well, all
  I'll tell you is it was a day of a sign for all of us
  to UNITE!

Oscar Guzman
Age: 12

A SCARY VISITOR

Once upon a chilly, dreary night,
I was upstairs alone reading a book on fright,
When suddenly there was a cold tap on my front door,
and I, weak and weary, said
"There's just someone at my door.
No more than that, nothing more."
But I myself was curious as can be,
for who would be knocking
on a frightening night like this?

As I walked down each stair,
they moaned and creaked as if they didn't care,
I could hear my heart pumping,
because I didn't know something,
who was tapping at my front door?
When I finally crept to the door, I felt like I hadn't slept,
and there was a chill that went up my spine,
when I suddenly heard the clock strike nine.

"Let's see who is at my front door," I thought,
"before I can take it no more."
And as I slowly opened the door,
I saw a grim, ghastly ghost who just replied,
"Dead men tell no tales."
And I cried and asked, "What do you mean?"
and the ghost answered, "You'll never be seen."
And with that I slammed the door,
rushed upstairs and talked no more.

I then went right to bed,
thinking of what the ghost just said.
"I hope I'll be able to sleep," I thought,
"for this is making me weep."

Christopher J. Meehan
Age: 13

ESCAPE THE SHADOWS

Lie yet worship
the fate
in which we rely on,
shielding the shadows
from us all,
still were unknown
to the heavens,
and the gods that conduct them.
Throughout time
we have formed
into monsters,
getting closer
to the release of
the darkness
crusading,
below us,
they somehow
survive.

Brad Carter
Age: 13

THE BREEZE

I felt the cool breeze
That made my knees really freeze
I am gonna sneeze

Danielle Flannigan
Age: 12

HEARTBROKEN

Heartbroken sits in a faded room,
On the floor in a dark, dimmed corner.
Heartbroken has despair painted on her face.
Her tears run down,
Just like a waterfall.
Heartbroken wears torn-up black jeans,
With a long hideous brown shirt,
She goes around with hair ripped out.
Not even close to a smile.
Eyes are swollen and dark.
Her cheeks are wrinkled,
Red from all the tears.
She hardly breathes at all.
Heartbroken feet are all torn up and bleeding,
From all the glass
She had broken.
She thinks life is over.
She is heartbroken!

Courtney Grinchuk
Age: 13

I AM FROM

I am from ice cream with my dad.
Pizza with my mom and mac and cheese with my family.
I am from playing the Wii in the basement,
doing homework in the kitchen,
and going on Facebook in the basement.
I am from dirt biking with my dad,
camping with my family,
and playing with my dog Mr. Pibb.
I am from Flight into Phoenix with my brother,
WORLD'S FASTEST INDIAN with my dad,
and A DIARY OF A WIMPY KID by Jeff Kinney
I am from hearing do your homework with my mom.
I am from seeing Columbia clothing with my mom.
I am from Catholic with my family.
I am from going to the Harley Davidson dealer
on the motorcycle with my dad.
And going to Smoky Hollow camping ground
with friends and family.
I am from when my grandfather died.
And when the H1N1 flu broke out.
I am from Puerto Rico with my mom
and Cuba with my dad.

Alejandro Del Castillo
Age: 12

The wet, cold snowflakes
Fly through the cold winter wind
As kids throw snowballs

Alexis Lamberti
Age: 11

Football games are fun
You can play it all year 'round
Even if it's cold

Alexandra Masnica
Age: 11

HATRED

Eyes are piercing, mean, haggard black,
White turns to ruby,
Mouth is a slash of crimson,
Veins popping out
Lightning statics through his body,
Leaking out of his fingers
Madness baking in his body,
Feels like someone stabbing him
And won't stop
Cannot handle the anger

Jordan Steiner
Age: 13

GUESS?

Here is something for you to guess
I promise it won't make your brain a mess.
They are really smart.
They can point to a number on a chart.
They can jump through hoops.
While they're doing loops.
They'll amaze you with their tricks.
As the clock ticks.
You won't notice the time it ends.
As they make you their friends.
They squeak to talk
Oh look I think one just walked!
Look at these amazing creatures
They could be teachers!
I don't really want to go
But it is the end of the show
They also eat fish out of bins
Did you guess what they are?

snihplod er'yeht

Gabriela Yañez Ortiz
Age: 11

SHADOWS OF THE NIGHT

As I walked through the halls of my forsaken house
I saw a dark figure in the distance
Instantly a feeling of danger swept throughout my body
Giving me emotions, I could not explain
I looked left and right and saw before me
A house I do not know anymore,
A house that has abandoned me
Once a warm abode, now an unfamiliar place
I took a few quivering steps
While shuddering in the breeze
Afraid of what was to come,
Afraid of what was near
The figure was moving, making no noise
Only making gestures I could not understand
It was clear there was someone hiding
In the dark shadows of my home
But do not fret, I thought
It is only a figment of my gloomy imagination
Slowly I walked towards it
Closer and closer
The closer I got, the clearer it became
And the more petrified it made me
The strange figure was that of a small child
Running around
Happy; joyful
One with a bright future, unlike myself
Then, the child fell into a deep, lifeless sleep
Looking closely at his face, I realized the child was me

That was the child I once had been
I had become a new person
One that I never thought I would be
And I realized, I don't know who I am anymore
This world has changed me
But "It's all in the past," I said aloud
"It's all in the past."
Then the small child opened his eyes
And uttered the words
"It's not too late"
The words echoed through my brain
While we vanished with the shadows of the night

Crystle Grinen
Age: 13

Rock music
loud, electric guitars
driving, singer, playing
Eddie Van Halen, Taylor Swift
soft, sad, cowboys
yodeling, trains, recording
Country music

Zachery O'Dowd
Age: 9

RECESS

Kids screaming at the top of their lungs.
Kids running in the scorching afternoon.
Kids playing tag.
Bell rings kids start running.
Then silence.

Karson Stricker
Age: 11

FRIEND

Strength, endurance
Kindness, reassurance
A message to send,
This is a friend.

They have seen
What you have been
They know of your likeness.

They very well might
Like what you like,
But they show their own brightness.

Sometimes your own age,
They're on your same page
This is a friend.

Steven Russell
Age: 13

O' class, o' class you are the best class ever.
Our teacher loves us,
because we do our best in class.
We listen, learn, and have fun.
But I'd rather be playing in the sun.

Cole Heintzelman

TEACHER'S LIST

Teaches multiplication $50 \times 50 = 2,500$.
Keeps students busy.
Teaches prayers.
Organizes a supply list.
Goes to church.
Does recess duty.
Takes us to gym class.
Shows kindness.
Grades papers.
Helps others.
Teaches.
Writes on chalkboard.
Role model.
Shows movies.
I can't believe the teacher does this all in one day.

Alex Burr

OCEAN OF LIES

A faint projection
Of light on the floor
Casts a fake sense of protection
The waves crash the rocky shore

The silence is broken
All alone, like a deflated beach ball
An unwanted truth is spoken
The answers call

Sand in my short hair
Sand in between my toes
This truth makes me feel bare
The morning fog glows

Whispers no more
The truth is out from behind the fog
Behind the flesh, behind the door
Paralyzed, stiff as a log

Thoughts and emotions
Rattling around
Appalled by this notion
But seeping no sound

Your words are true
But cruelly so
Secrets hidden below the salty blue
Turning friend to foe

You leave as quietly as you came
Making my lips quiver
Making me point the blame
Leaving me alone to shiver

Contemplating and relating
The unknown finally revealed
My hatred fading
True feelings concealed

I take it in
Look out of my mind
Be adventurous, like Huck Finn
Cutting off my bind

Instead of trudging
I lightly skip
Assumptions slowly budging
A smile on the edge of my lip

Kathryn Teberg

HORSES

H andsome animals
O pen minded
R un freely in the meadows
S un is shining on their silky backs
E very single one is loving and caring
S ome are bigger . . . some smaller . . . all are loved.

Cosette Nawrocki
Age: 11

IF I COULD FLY

If I could fly, I'd fly so high.
If I could fly, I'd fly and fly
until I reached
the bright blue sky.
If I could fly,
I'd say hi to all the sea gulls
in the sky.
I'd fly and fly
and fly all day,
I'd fly and fly
so far away,
past my house, past all the trees,
even oceans and big blue seas.
I'd feel so happy
and light with glee.
I'd fly and fly
and fly all day,
but that's a lot of work
I'd say.
Then I'd go home and munch away
on pizza, cookies, and all that they
have left over in the fridge today.
Now I'm very excited for the next day
when I get up and fly away.

Caroline Martin
Age: 9

OLD NAVY

Old Navy Old Navy
It rhymes with old gravy.
There once was a boy named Davey,
Who shopped at Old Navy.
He didn't like to shop at Old Navy.
He found everything too wavy.

Garrett Sode

FREE

All I feel is the rain stinging my skin
and the moist ground under my feet,
All I hear is the babbling stream and the rustling leaves,
All I see is the mist parting
to welcome the warmth of the sun,
All I smell is the autumn leaves and the fresh pine,
No longer do I feel trapped as a bird in a cage,
No longer do I hear car horns and chattering people,
No longer do I see black roads and tall buildings,
No longer do I smell putrid gas and choking fumes,
Free as the chirping and hooting birds am I,
Free as the howling and barking wolf am I,
Free as the whistling and bellowing wind am I,
Free as the swift and flowing rivers am I,
I am free.

Danika Rose Whitcomb
Age: 11

YOU CAN'T WRITE A POEM
ABOUT A SKINNED KNEE

You can't write a poem about a skinned knee.
It would be bruised and scraped,
Something not at all attractive in appearance.
And it would probably be bloody, too,
Meaning there would be a bloody mess everywhere,
Which you would have to clean up.

You can't write a poem about a skinned knee,
Because there's bound to be a lot of crying.
And if there was crying you'd need to have a Kleenex
And one Kleenex would lead to two
Then three
Then four
Then maybe a whole box.

You can't write a poem about a skinned knee
Because then you'd need to find a Band-Aid.
And if you had to find a Band-Aid
You might end up needing two
Or three
Or four
Or maybe even five.

You can't write a poem about a skinned knee,
It's getting too expensive!
Kleenex and Band-Aids
Bloody messes and unpleasant feelings in your stomach
And I really do hope you aren't going to faint.
Really, wouldn't you just rather not write a poem at all?

You can't write a poem which
Might hurt very suddenly,
And then hurts when you clean it,
And hurts every single time you move it
And just won't stop hurting.
Until you wake up one day . . .
And realize it's gone!

Margaret E. Gawlik
Age: 17

MICE

I have a mouse.
The mouse lives in my house.
He nibbles on cheese.
When he runs out,
For more he begs, please, please, PLEASE!!
He has a hole in the wall
It is in the hall.
We scream when we see him,
Although he is nice.
And I think instead of mouse,
It should be mice!
I think it should be mice because,
My family has caught a lot.
He runs across my countertop.
He's a gray little mouse,
And the gray little mouse,
Lives in my house.

Hannah Baird
Age: 10

IT'S JANUARY

The poppers pop
At 12:00 a.m. sharp
The candles flicker
Atop my birthday cake
The crowds cheer
For the final touchdown
Get jazzed it's January

Susie places that last button eye
on Frosty's face, while her parents shovel
the sopping wet snow off the sidewalk.
Bobby gets up from his perfect snow angel.
Get your jackets it's January

Cathy arrives at her New Year's Eve party,
Fashionably late of course,
Wearing her silver sparkly dress.
While sipping her champagne
She looks around to see
Who will receive that midnight kiss.
Get jealous it's January

Emily sticks out her tongue
To catch those falling flakes.
She finishes her figure eight
And goes to get some cocoa
That her mother so nicely makes.
Get joyful it's January

It's that crazy-cold time
That blizzardy-bold time.
It's that spectacular-snow time
That fireplace-glow time.
Join us it's January

Michelle O'Driscoll
Age: 17

MOM

Caring, helping, loving Mom
You're as smart as cars
and as smart as a computer
Your black hair can look like a black hole
but it reminds me you care
You might yell louder than thunder
but it is for my own good
You work all day and I don't do as much for you
Without you my life would be harder than it is now
Hugging, working, helping
Joking, laughing, having fun
Making food with love and care
Shopping, concerts, and watching Filipino shows
Playing games with my brothers
Black hair, dark brown eyes all remind me of you
I might not show it but I really love you
I'm lucky to have you as my mom.

Judd Ivan Palonpon

TYSON

Terrorizing the house until
we put him outside.
Barking at the neighbors oh, my!
Call him back inside.
Time to practice my baritone.
Tyson be quiet!
Now he's barking
and putting his head in the bell
and howling.
Time to go to sleep Tyson move over!
Won't budge a bit
I push as hard as I can,
no good.
Put him in the basement
for the night.
The next morning he comes
out all wound up and ready
to go terrorize the town.
Instead I give him a hug
because I love my Boston Terrier.

Nadia Merida
Age: 10

LUCK

Luck has a confident face,
With glistening obsidian hair,
A cracked grin and shining bright eyes,
In his green suit and black pants,
He walks to a slot machine
Without a single worry on his face,
He pulls the lever just perfectly,
The slots all stop, each on 777,
Thousands of coins shoot out
Of the machine,
He shows a smile of satisfaction,
And walks away without
Touching a single one.

Zachary Konecki
Age: 12

GALAXY

The glistening sky is filled with many secrets.
It starts with a little planet and grows and grows.
The galaxy is a big place so you know,
You better not be a lost man or you'll be a dead man.
If you wish on a wishing star anywhere in the world
it's said it will come true.
So wish you may and wish you might
before it passes through.

Gabrielle A. Weaver
Age: 11

DECEMBER

The ground—covered in a blanket of white
The trees—sprinkled with flurries
It's that time of the year
Where children run around with their tongues out
Catching snowflakes
Building snowmen
Making snow angels

The aroma of sweet ginger and peppermint
  is traveling through the house
Grandma is baking gingerbread cookies
Mom is checking on the nasty fruitcake
  that everyone will despise
Little Jeremy is shaking his Christmas presents
Guessing
Wondering
Hoping
Impatiently waiting for the arrival of Christmas

A woman in a red pea coat,
  bundled up from her head to her toe
Hustles and bustles the slippery streets of Chicago,
  her hands filled with bags
She passes the delightfully decorated store windows
She passes the happy faces
  ice-skating in Millenium Park
She passes the other frantic busybodies
  shopping and rushing

It's wintry-wonder
It's crazy-cold
It's cheerful-carols
It's December!

A little girl in a pretty pink dress
Lights the menorah with her father
Her brother sits in the family room
Spinning the Dreidel with their mother
'Round and 'round that Dreidel goes
Clearly made of clay
As Hanukkah happiness fills the home
For eight nights in a row

Holiday music everywhere
Boots from left and right
Scarves
And hats
And gloves
And coats
It's freezing cold outside
It's that wonderful time
Where winter's in the air
Before the New Year comes alive

Maria A. Di Vietro
Age: 18

CHILLS

Chills are in my spine
Cold wind whispers in the night
Cold November chills

Dominik Zawartko
Age: 11

THE GIRL WITH A CURLED WIG
AND THE PIG, JIG, AND FIGS

There is a girl
Who has some curls
The girl has curls in her wig
And is also doing some type of jig
The girl does a jig with a pig
There is a tree of figs
The pig is doing a jig with a tree of figs
The girl is also there doing a jig with a pig
And the pig is doing a jig with a tree of figs
The wig is also very big
The wig also has curls
Which is on the girl
And the girl's name is Pearl
And she has on the wig of curls

Treshur McDonald

WAITING FOR MY BIRTHDAY

Everybody has a birthday.
Mine is one day away.
I cannot wait to play!
I am very excited because I am turning nine.
November 20 is all mine.
Turning nine will be so much fun.
When will this day ever be done?
Every day is one less day.
It's almost time for me to play.
I just can't wait.
It's almost time to
CELEBRATE!!

Katelyn Hopp

MY HAMSTER

My hamster's name is Frito.
His best friend is Dorito.
He is as small as a little leaf.
His feet get stuck on carpets.
He gets up early in the morning.
His cage is always a mess.
He likes to go in the grass.

Sydney Eberhart

MATH

Math is fun, math is cool
We are no fool

Have some pi
With these rhymes

Live equations
No quotations

Collect some money
I know it's funny

Measure some food
It will end up tasting very good

Do some fractions
Instead of captions

Quack up some facts

If that makes sense
Count some cents

And if in doubt
Read and find out
If that helps
Tell me what the frustration is all about!!

Salvador Rodriguez
Age: 11

SPRING

See colored flowers
Raining, muddy, wait for sun
Outside many worms

Armin Ward
Age: 11

SHOOTING STARS

Shooting stars twinkling
Brightly shining in my eyes
Quickly make a wish

Katiemarie Owen
Age: 10

KYLE ETHAN

I have a brother named Kyle.
Sometimes Kyle makes a pile.
It might take awhile for Kyle to pick up the pile.
Sometimes the pile is on tile.
What happens if there is a pile of paper?
Would I have to file for a while with my brother Kyle?

Laci La Placa

A DAY'S LIMIT

Numerous songs can be sung,
Many people can be met,
Several sights can be seen,
Plenty of things can be said.

Every moment is a new experience,
Taking every step without delay,
Trying to enjoy everything around,
But you can do so much in one day.

Ethan Vargas
Age: 13

TEACHERS

Teachers teachers teachers
have lots and lots of features
They may be nice they may be mean
but in the school they're everywhere to be seen
They have punishments like time-outs
and some kids shout and pout
They teach subjects like English and reading
and before you know it you're succeeding!
You know how you feel on the first day of school
but if you're nervous then you're a fool
because teachers feel the same way too!

David Fang
Age: 9

MOMS

Moms are special.
Moms are great.
Moms know how to fix mistakes.
Moms know how to fix a frown.
She simply turns it upside down.
She makes me laugh and always smile.
She always goes that extra mile.
I love my mom deep in my heart.
She keeps my family from falling apart.

Jake Winchell

VIDEO GAMES

Video games are cool and fun
They are great for everyone
From sports, action, and war too
And some kids games too.

So when I turn on the game
It's time for me to relax
I can sit on my brown chair
Or lie on my back
Either way it's all good to me
Now leave me alone in peace.

Brandon Roberts
Age: 11

MUSIC

It pours
In and out of
My soul

Wakes my
Mind
And heart

Images
Scatter in my
Mind

And sparkles
In my eyes

You hear rock,
Country, the blues,
And jazz

I hear a pleasing
Mood that
Settles my soul
When I'm frustrated
Or even depressed

You may hear a
Sibling off-tune
I hear a sibling
Keeping their
Mind off work

You hear a mother
Slow in her words
I hear a mother

Soothing a child
Who shudders
From a nightmare

And yes that's music
To me

Sami Dyer
Age: 16

MY FAMILY

My family is very, very fun.
They are even more cooler than a bun.
They are nice to me.
But they are tough as a tree.
Bossy and mean
Or nice like a queen.
Boring and plain
Just like a cane.
But even though they are boring sometimes.
They are also fun and sometimes fine.
But one thing for sure,
I love them no kidding, no pure.

Abdiel Munoz

MY SISTERS

I love my sisters
They are not misters
They are so nice
We're afraid of mice
We talk a lot
Sometimes we play dots
We sympathize
When someone cries
And in the summer
When it rains it's a bummer
We go to the stores
It's not a bit bored
We shop for cool stuff
We can't get enough
And when we come home
We grab all our phones
We separate
And when it's late
We all go downstairs
And braid all our hairs
And then it is night
We go out of sight
Sisters are cool
They do not drool.

Michelle Bednarowski

DADS ARE GREAT

I think my dad is really cool
I love to play with him at the pool
We really like to play fun games
We also make up silly names
He always plays the music loud
And especially the song "Boom Boom Pow!"
I love my dad, I love him so,
Especially when my dad says no!

Bailee Winchell

ODE TO MANATEES

Oh, manatees
Oh, manatees
How you're so fat and gray
I would love to have you as a pet but that's not OK.
You live in the ocean
You eat algae and plants
Your whiskers so long
You're as cute as can be
I love you so much
You're the cutest one in the sea
Oh, manatees
Oh, manatees
You are the best

Alexa Zonta

SPRING

Spring is here
And the sky is clear.
The sun is out
And our flowers will sprout.
These are the signs of spring.

Teens on bikes
And babies on trikes.
Scooters fly by
And joggers say hi.
These are the signs of spring.

Grills are smoking
And the corn is soaking.
Keep the grill steady
And get the butter ready.
These are the signs of spring.

Open your doors
And clean your floors.
Dust bunnies have to go
So get on your knees and dust real low.
These are the signs of spring.

Spring is here
And summer is near.
Winter has passed
And spring is here at last!

Zack Baumgartner

SPRING IS HERE!

Peonies are pink
Violets are blue.
Springtime is here.
The sky is blue with puffy white clouds.
The grass is green, the flowers are blooming.
All of my friends shout Hurray! Hurray!
They all shout as they play outside.
For you know I am thankful
that the brutal winter days are over.
And so I am happy that spring is here!

Madeline Burke

MY TEACHER, MRS. BENJAMIN

She is caring.
She is nice.
She helps me if I need it.

She's by my side.
All the time.
No matter what happens, she still cares for me.
We're all one big class family because of her.

We all work together good because of her.
Who is she? Mrs. Benjamin!

Mackenzie Prusko

YOU

The last time I saw you,
I began to cry.
A kiss on the cheek,
Was a final good-bye.
A farewell to you,
Was hard to do,
But I know you'll be up in Heaven,
With a better view.
The memories I have,
Are still very clear to me,
Whether you came here to Chicago
Or we spent a summer at Honey Bee.
You're my papa
And I will always be,
You were someone in my life,
That meant so much to me.
You're now asleep forever,
Never will you wake,
I'll always think about you,
And my heart will continue to ache.
I miss you so much,
And love you too,
I still shed a tear every time I think about you.

Tori Iatarola
Age: 13

ODE TO MILK

You don't make me happy
You don't make me sad
But when I drink you
I'm frequently glad.
Your glistening whiteness
Your cold crispy taste
You are the best drink
That someone could taste
You aren't as fizzy as soda
And you're not as cool as Yoda
But when I have debates
On which milk or Yoda
I'd pick milk any day
Because I'm sorry to say
That I don't like Star Wars
But I would drink milk
Any day.

Sydney Ryan

There once was a monkey.
He danced really funky.
He met a bee named Sonney
That had lots of honey.
That's why he is very hunky!

Rebecca Aguilar

COLORS

When I see red,
I see an apple just picked on a fall day.

When I see purple,
I see a blanket cozy and warm.

When I see pink,
I see a mat on the porch.

When I see green,
I see a big tree waving to everyone who passed me.

When I see white,
I see a happy cloud dancing in the sky.

When I see blue,
I see a bluebell flower swaying in the breeze.

Morgan Jones

SKY

Lightning bolts flying
One by one and two by two
Cloud art in the air

Alex Wiedemann
Age: 11

THE FOX

There once was a big fox.
He liked to eat a big ox.
They would like to fight,
In the crazy night.
Then they had the chickenpox.

Caden Valera

EMOTIONS

let me be sad
let me cry
let me be happy
let me smile

let me be frustrated
let me think
let me be curious
let me search

let me be angry
let me growl
let me think freely
let me have emotions

Madison Ricke
Age: 10

FINALLY SPRING!

Spring is here!
Time to cheer!
The sun is here to shine.
The flowers look so divine.
The spring is all mine. Hope you have fun!
It will be fun in the sun.
The grass is green and bright.
I want to play, play until day turns to night!

Riley Kenney

SPRING

I really do like spring.
It is my favorite thing.
It's the time to have fun,
Or play or run.
There's rabbits hopping high,
And clouds up in the sky.
You can ride our bike,
Or go on a long hike.
Then it stops snowing,
And flowers start growing.
That's what happened in spring,
Which is my favorite thing.

Jimmy Knapp

HALLEY'S COMET

Halley's Comet is big and bright,
In the sky one fall night.
Comet Halley visits every seventy-five years,
When it arrives, everyone cheers!
In fifty years, Halley will fly by
I'll be watching the clear night sky.

Hailey Bruno

VETERANS

Loving veterans give freedom to us,
They risk their lives for America.

They changed the world by what they have done,
They risked their lives for everyone.

Some of them in war have passed away,
So we can all be here today.

I'm so glad they did what is right
They all risked their lives to give us a safe life.

I am so happy that they gave up their time
To give us our freedom and make the U.S.A. shine.

Kier Alimario

MY DAD'S OLD CAR

He names his car Lar
He'll hoist me up
And nudge me in
He says "let the jubilee begin"
Dad has scruples for driving
And for high-fiving
But definitely not for car cleaning
His car is always leaving
That yucky car stink
Makes my face turn pink
The unremitting smell
Makes me want to yell
My dad as a tour guide
Makes undulating rides
It's not a tranquil scene
I'm not trying to be mean
Low rate for rejuvenation
Runs out of gas before your location
My dad's eccentric car
The car named Lar
He'll love it forever
Under any weather
It always makes me smile
He'll be around for a while

Elise Deremer

MUSIC

Music—the best way to express feelings
From the solid gold oldies
To the hip-hop today
So much fun to listen to
So much love
So much hate
So much peace
Music . . . so many memories

Jake Lafrenz
Age: 12

SPRING IS HERE!

Spring is here!
Everyone dance and everyone cheer!
Flowers are blooming.
The sky is blue.
The birds are tweeting and so are you.
They play in the sun and swing set too!
They swing on the swings and jump rope too!
But right now I'm inside because I've got the flu.
There are flies in here
Shoo! Shoo!
Shoo! Shoo!

Emma Warnke

MY TEACHER

My teacher is so cool.
You will never ever want to drool.
She is nice, but hates mice.
You will want her for a teacher.

Megan Moylan
Age: 9

BLANK

Blank mind,
Nothing in it,
No thoughts,
No feeling,
No desire,
Nothing.
Trying to think,
But nothing's there,
I'm just a shell,
Nothing inside,
No emotion,
Lifeless,
Tranquility,
This nothingness brings peace.
No regrets,
No care,
Nothing
Is happiness,
Pure happiness.

Shazia Siddiqui
Age: 13

THE DANDELION AND THE ROSE

You grow in a precious land made just for you
I am accompanied by a weed or two

You have perfect petals soft and red
Mine easily shed

People are dazed by your beauty
I'm often accompanied by an achhoooooey

Your odor is alluring
Mine quite repelling

However you cause red goo
When someone tries to pick you

I may not be beautiful
But I am not harmful

You rot quite easily
When out of your luxury

I thrive to continue growing
And avoid a lawn mowing

You may be more attracting
But I am more hardworking

I guess we are even
But just for the time being

Manasa Datla
Age: 12

A TRUE STORY

A puppy runs through the grass
I must catch her but she's too fast

I have one chance to get her home
And it's a risk I must take alone

She is in danger, and I am too
That is why I must catch her soon

She is a Doberman no more than one
I guess she's too young to know this isn't fun

Then, down my face, the tears started flowing
As soon as I caught sight of where she was going

The highway grew nearer, and so did the end of my time
When she crossed the side of the ditch filled with grime

Her paws hit the pavement and I stopped in a panic
My heart sunk faster than the Titanic

"Ellie STOP!" I yelled at her
She just weaved through the cars like she hadn't heard

I ran up and down the side of the street sadly
When a woman opened her door to greet Ellie gladly

I jumped over the hood and quickly snatched her
I thanked the woman with eyes teary and blurred

I still look back on that day
And I am still thankful that Ellie and I are alive today

Lauren Guske
Age: 14

I LOVE

My grandma's shrimp with breading.
Riding my bike.
Snowball fights.
Motorbikes.
Baking moist chewy brownies.
The Bears football team.
Bella, my kitten.
Saki, my dog.
Lila, my dog.
Lobster and crab with sweet butter.
Salmon.
School.
Vanilla cupcakes with sweet creamy frosting.
Climbing really, really tall trees.
Snowboarding.
Six Flags Great America.
Coffee.
Big time rush.

Sydney Williams

THE WHITE DOG

My dog is white.
He has a short height.
He is scared of big heights.
He likes short heights.
He runs off big heights.

Sam Cesario
Age: 8

SHADY TREE

There is one tree
That I sit under
While the sky is blue
And there is no thunder

The tree is oak
And full of leaves
That's home to birds
But has no bees

As I read my book
And go to sleep
The little birds
Go Peep, Peep, Peep

As each day passes
One by one
I think of you shady tree
When the day is done

Elizabeth Clements
Age: 12

POND WATERS

There is a small pond
There are ducks, geese, frogs, and toads
There is no water

Mitchell Willman
Age: 11

THE MAGIC OF AN ORDINARY OBJECT

Take an object
Any object
An ordinary object
A piece of paper
Treasure it
Hold it
Write on it
Dance with it
Do what you want with it
The magic of an ordinary object
Use it
Feel it
Embrace it
Enjoy it
You hear a voice:
The magic of an ordinary object . . .
Is in your hands.

Lauren Desch

WHERE INSPIRATION HIDES FOR ME

Inspiration hides under my pillow,
where the Tooth Fairy once stopped to rest.
Inspiration creeps under my bed,
where my best nightmares sleep.
Inspiration floats in the ever-changing clouds,
where the angels slumber.
Inspiration echoes in the never-ending hall
of two mirrors facing each other.
Inspiration shines in the gleam
of my stuffed animals' eyes when I hug them.
Inspiration snuggles under my cat
when he is curled up in front of the cauldron.
Inspiration gathers in the musty costumes
of my former self.
Inspiration radiates within the glow of a firefly,
where every garden fairy is born.
Inspiration skulks in the blood-red Harvest Moon
of October.
Inspiration lies in the odd jokers in each deck of cards,
cackling.
Inspiration sneaks in the shadow,
mimicking my every move.
Inspiration entwines itself in the silky thread
of a spider's web, catching in my hair.
Inspiration is revealed on Friday the thirteenth,
when the best storms brew.
Inspiration glows in the light of a jack-o'-lantern,
urging me to trick-or-treat there.
Inspiration reveals itself in the swirls of cream in my tea,
showing me things to come.
Inspiration blossoms in the flowers in the garden
where the bees rest their wings.

Inspiration spins in the inside of a watch,
turning this way and that.
Inspiration resonates in the strings of my baby grand,
where the souls of previous players sing.
Inspiration resides in the sugar skulls
that represent my ancestors.
Inspiration unfolds in my sanctum-sanctorum,
where my dreams become reality.

Brogan Crist
Age: 12

SOUNDS I FEAR

Certain sounds creep me out.
loud crashes
sirens at night
Other sounds make me still.
screams
breaking glass
the doorbell when I'm alone
Certain sounds arrest all thought.
barking dogs
fire alarms
gunshots
Other sounds stop my heart.
silence

Sarah Summers
Age: 12

THE BLUE SKY
The blue cloudy sky
The sky is getting darker
God made the nice sky

Jocelyn Barron
Age: 9

THE STABLES
The first time I walk into a stable
It does not relate to a storybook fable
It smells really bad
And it looks kind of sad
With all of the horses' shiny eyes
It looks as though they're about to cry
But then I walk to the horses' stalls
It makes me really want to bawl
As I look in their excited faces
And go in their tight embraces
The seed of connection is planted so
But the jewel of excitement is also, though
But they ignore the bright, shiny luster
And they stay away from the other cluster
Of the other horses playing around
And they wait for me to make a sound
Then I tell them hello
And stand next to them, way below
And I bring them out to see
The rest of the stable waiting for me

Izzy Richardson
Age: 11

AUTUMN THROUGH THE SENSES

Autumn sounds like
Loud screams from kids,
Wind whistling through my head,
Crumpling candy,
And suckers crushed by my teeth.

Autumn smells like
A roaring fire in the fireplace,
Misty fog hovering over the ground,
Turkey baking in the oven,
And fresh pumpkin pie on the counter.

Autumn feels like
Thin candy wrappers against my hand,
Brisk weather outside,
Rough tree bark,
And hard cement on the ground.

Autumn tastes like
Sugary candy from my basket,
Fluffy mashed potatoes in my mouth,
Salty pumpkin seeds on my tongue,
And wet leaves in my throat.

Autumn looks like
Red leaves on the ground,
Baskets filled with vegetables,
Kids in the bounce house at Fall Festival,
And fresh tomatoes off of the vine.

Aaron Perlman
Age: 10

CANDY BARK

Candy bark is good
Candy bark melts in your mouth
It fills you with joy

Seth Middleton DuBois Dickinson
Age: 11

MAGENTA

Magenta feels like a burning, crackling fire
in the fireplace,
Magenta tastes like a cold afterlife of dried out rose
in the winter months,
Magenta looks like my red mechanical pencil
drawing gracefully,

Magenta dreams of being everybody's favorite color,
Magenta imagines a big world
that is only magenta in the summer
and pink in the winter,
Magenta hopes that she will not be mixed in with green
when being painted,

Magenta is a far-away planet rotating in space,
Magenta is the bright ideas you get,
Magenta is a new, beautiful, blooming flower in Florida.

Rebecca Rossen
Age: 10

THANK YOUS TO WRITE

The week after Christmas is a fright
For I have many thank yous to write.

So many, so many
Thank yous to write.

One to Aunt Mary Loop
For my orange and blue Hula-Hoop
One to Grandma Macaroni
For my black polka-dotted pony

So many, so many
Thank yous to write

Two to Auntie Lara and Uncle Louse
For the bike and Barbie dollhouse.
One to Cousin Mandy
For all the Halloween candy

Too many, too many
Thank yous to write

Can I do them all?
All one hundred forty-three thank yous?
Can I do them?
Nope!
I don't have enough envelopes!

Olivia Willrett
Age: 10

119

THE PERFECT HUNT HORSE

I need to find a horse to hunt
The perfect hunt horse
A pony
A horse
A draft
Size is not an issue
Nothing could make this situation worse!
I need a horse
And I need one NOW!
A horse that will
Run without a hesitation
A horse that doesn't care
If it's blistering hot
Or if it's numbing cold
A horse that knows
When to go
And when to whoa
I need a horse
And I need one
NOW!

I know exactly where to go
To the stable
Down to the second row
First stall on the right
With the label
Huckleberry

I had forgotten of the very most absolute
Perfect horse to hunt
That I already know and love so much
He is big
He is broad
He is the only one I see
He is the one I need
He is the right horse for me

My horse Huckleberry
Is my perfect horse to hunt

Emily Lorenz
Age: 12

THE BEACH

Splashing waves crashing on the warm beach.
Kids are playing and some babies screech.
People listening to the beach band.
Grownups tanning in the warm sand.
People laying in the blinding hot sun.
People packing things because night has begun.
Crying kids are very sad to go.
Though they cannot wait 'til it will snow.

Audrey Yaus
Age: 10

TREE

Look at the dry bark.
It will have many leaves soon.
Spring is coming soon.

Audrey Kessler
Age: 7

ANGER

Bundled up in a dark corner
Anger wears a black shirt and pants
Thoughts muddled up in her mind
With nobody around
Frightened off by her bitterness
Her eyes have a twitch in them
With a smirk on her face
Every time she talks
Smoke comes out of her ears
Big black tattered boots
Torn when she is angry
Her eyes are blown up like big balloons
Within her dark surroundings
She is angry!

Courteney Giuffre
Age: 12

I AM

I am from softballs, skateboards, and teen magazines.
I am from too many posters in my room
and climbing on my loft bed.
I am from orchids in the window sill,
fake flowers on the glass.

I am from people who care about their heritage
from short and loud,
Elizabeth, Jeffrey, and the Dacanays and the Hillards.

I am from the gossipers and lovers.
From I love you so much and turn down your music.
I am from the trust of God and going to church
but not every Sunday.
I am from the Philippines, rice and puntset.

I am from the time I fell on my skateboard,
and when my brother hit his head on the wall.
I am from photo albums showing me with my messy hair,
my little dogs that passed away,
and fun times I have with my loving family.

Olivia Moore
Age: 11

I am from video games from XBOX
And building blocks from Lego.
I am from the hidden white house on the block,
And the tree in my backyard.
I am from mayday baskets and freckled skin
From Farrell, Clint, and Molly.

I am from shyness and hollering.
From don't go to bed too late
And stop eating so much before dinner.
I am from going to church on Sunday.

I am from Geneva and Ireland,
Corned beef and cabbage.
From my dad throwing old light bulbs off a cliff
To make gunshot noises,
The riding through the flower bed,
And the seven arms my brother broke himself.

I am from my house where the wall is covered
With pictures of family,
Friends,
And the best moments in our lives.

Stephen Lewis
Age: 11

I am from jumping dogs,
From Country Time lemonade and Dominick's pizza.
I am from the blue house with chipping paint,
And the rolling of ankles on walnuts
I am from the cherry tree,
And the bright moon shining through my window

I am from the Thanksgiving walks and athletes,
From Carey and McKinney
I am from the clowns
And people who want to do things without any help
From your eyes are bigger than your stomach
And make some lemonade

I am from gospel and hymns
I am from CDH and Germany
From pie and fudge
I am from the mom who could have been a track star
An awesome cook who is my dad
I am from books full of pictures,
Drawers packed with memories,
But most of all these things mean so much to me

Tai Bibbs
Age: 10

I am from teen pop posters
From J-14 and BOP magazines.
I am from the ceiling in my bedroom
Where I spend most of my time listening to music
And doing homework.

I am from family daily dinners and prayers,
From my mom, dad, and our Venen name.
I am from the outdoors, enjoying nature and bike riding,
From my Great-grandma Lill's red hair color
And my mom's freckles.
I am from Illinois, Irish and Polish ancestry,
From spaghetti and pizza.

I am from the hands of my brother
Playing Star Wars Two with me,
From family rummy, speed, and hearts,
My favorite card games
I am from storage boxes of albums of pictures,
Bead arts, and crafts.

I am from memories of my family vacations,
My grandma's Michigan home, and family time
Making my memories of good moments each day.

Sarah Marie Venen
Age: 11

ADVENTURE

What is adventure?
A way of being free in the world
You get to see life from other people's perspective
You take risks
For the good
And for the bad
Seeing life as one
People, animals, plants working as one
New ideas big and small
New people, new life, and new opportunities
Adventures are wild
And can be very dangerous
We live adventure as it lasts
Then put the rest in the past
We fall, we cry, we will have bad days
But until you live adventure you will
Always cry at the same things
Always have bad days
But with this thing called adventure
We can ALL explore
So before it's your time
Take an adventure

Kaitlyn C. Pearson
Age: 12

S weet
I ntelligent
S illy
T rusting
E verlasting
R ambunctious
S pecial

Paige Mosher
Age: 10

I am from knickknacks, from loose papers
  and shoe stacks,
From eight full Gatorade bottles,
From twisted bamboo plants and a Xango salesman,
I am from the family with the only red truck.
I am from the pepper plant and the cactus.
I am from Cinco de Mayo and black hair,
From Adan and Areli and the Villa family
I am from the social and united,
From be nice and use your manners
I am from Catholics and Dupage, and Mexico
From the time my dad almost lost his finger at work
And the time my cousin paddled a little too far out
In Lake Michigan
I am from that picture album
With photos since I was born.

Victor Villa
Age: 11

WATCHING

Wisps of cotton balls float in the sky
Drifts of glitter sparkle by
Bright sparks of light amuse you
While you see it come through
Picture shapes inside your head
As you lie in a cool, green bed
Watching the bright blue sky
Really makes time fly

Laura Masnato
Age: 12

THE BIG BROWN EYES

When I look at her, and she looks at me,
I know she's telling me something
And somehow I understand,
In her eyes I see love and laughter,
I see squirrels, and rabbits,
I see the cat,
But most of all I see loyalty, and pride,
There is so much more than meets the eye,
It's like the never-ending sky,
There's never any lies,
In her big brown eyes.

Victoria J. Teik
Age: 11

THE WISE OLD OWL HOOTS

A baby is born,
Wailing as it comes to life,
And the wise old owl hoots.

The baby grows into a boy,
A boy that loves nature,
While the wise old owl hoots.

The boy grows into a man,
Making his own decisions,
While the wise old owl hoots.

Black as night,
Bright as day,
The wise old owl hoots,
And watches,
As the man grew into a husband.

Then the husband grew into a father,
The baby wailing as it came to life,
And the wise old owl hooted,
And hooted,
And hooted.

The father grew into a grandfather,
And the wise old owl hooted and watched,
Watched and hooted.

One night,
The grandfather left forever,
Never to return to Earth,
And the wise old owl hooted,
And hooted,
And hooted,
For the very last time.

Not far away a young owl was born,
Not wailing as it came to life,
But hooting,
Because this young owl would grow and grow,
So the hooting of the wise old owl would live.

When a child is born,
Wailing as it comes to life,
The wise old owl will hoot,
And hoot,
And hoot.

Rose Aubery
Age: 12

M uscle
U nstoppable when running at full speed
S team slowly rolls out of their nostrils
T ougher than nails
A nticipate to catch them
N aturally beautiful
G oing as fast as the wind

Naomi Nichols
Age: 12

MY POODLE WILL NOT EAT HIS NOODLES

My poodle will not eat his noodles.
He eats his rice like cats chase mice.
When it is noodle time he runs under the couch.
He does not have to crouch.
I dream of the day he will ask for noodles.
That is the day I will make him a caboodle of noodles.

Olivia Gonzalez
Age: 10

Josh
Microscopic, brilliant, swift, creative
Sibling of Danny
Lover of hot summers, delicious Italian food,
confusing mathematics
Who feels content after eating,
exhausted after an excess of running,
slumbering in the morning
Who fears dark closed areas, slithering snakes,
and death
Who gives a positive attitude,
encouragement to friends, good advice
Who would like to see Ireland, a Hawaiian volcano,
the Amazon Rainforest
Resident of Illinois
Bowen

Joshua Thomas Burgess Bowen
Age: 10

LEAVES

The autumn leaves are falling.
They're falling on your heads.
Leaves you're raking.
Leaves you're jumping in.
Leaves are everywhere.
Leaves are very colorful.
Leaves bring you great joy.
Fall is here and leaves are too.

Emily Murphy
Age: 10

WHERE I'M FROM

I am from a well-loved, second generation Snoopy doll,
a DS, and a red-satin ribbon.
I am from Nintendo, Sony, Sketchers, Lego,
and Lucasarts.
I am from a normal, red-brick, calm, and young house.
I am from the tall hickory trees in my backyard, the short,
plump, sergeant crab bushes, and an ivy wall.
I am from Sleepy Hollow, Thanksgiving with relatives,
and Christmas Eve at Grandma's house.
From "you'll shoot your eye out"
and that my brain would turn into mashed potatoes
from too much screens.
I'm from Park Ridge, IL, Lithuanian, Dutch, Polish,
German, and English.

Matthew Woelffer
Age: 11

DARKNESS

It can be scary!
Sometimes darkness is scary!
It is everywhere!

Oliver Green
Age: 8

ORANGE

Orange is a pumpkin
Orange is a goldfish fin

Orange is a bright sunset
Orange is a retriever that's wet

Orange is a tabby cat
Laying on an orange mat

Orange is a tiger
That's feasting on spiders

Orange is a carrot
And a part of a parrot

Orange is a maple leaf
Or a candy-corn thief

Anna Fortelka
Age: 7

WIND

Wind blows with the leaves
Wind is nice and cold it blows
Wind is nice and cold.

Eliot Moore
Age: 7

I am from a super-clean mom,
Mountain Dew, and centerpieces
I am from a light-green house
And from big pine trees

I am from Thanksgiving in Mexico and jokers
From Susan and Carl McGhee.
I am from laughing and funny
From make a better door than a window and bedhead
I am from I don't know what I believe about God

I am from CDH, Germany, and Ireland
Homemade macaroni and seafood
From the elbow my sister broke falling out of her chair
And from the time my mom fell off her horse
And woke up in the hospital
I am from the old pictures in our photo albums
Behind our chair
Under our bookshelf

David McGhee
Age: 11

135

I am from big messes
From canned fruit and mementos.

I am from the only brick house on the street.
I am from the roses and the long grass in the yard.

I am from getting a present
  even when it is not my special day
From long and wavy hair.

From Antonia Carmona Hoyos and Monroy Alatorre
  and Carmona
I am from the loving and the selfish.
From it is not hard if you think about it and think again.

I am from Catholic churches
  and charities to help the homeless.
I am from Mexico, Halapa, tamales, and flan.
From the Antionas branch, arros con leche,
  and from a grandma who enjoys spending time
  with us, her family.
I am from Mexico that means the world to me.

Lizeth Carmona
Age: 11

TREES

Trees are very bright.
Trees are very colorful.
Trees have leaves on them.

Lauren Winchell
Age: 7

PATRIOTIC

The eagle glides over the battlefield
Holding the American flag that has patriotism
Sewn in every stitch
Its razor-sharp claws hold the flag
Tightly for our nation
The eagle's brave hazel eyes and moon-bright head
Glisten in the sunlight
His strong brawny wings
Cut through the air as cannons fire through the enemy
The eagle's brick-strong beak opens and unleashes a cry,
A cry of victory, bravery, and valor
His true heart pounds
With fearlessness and audacity
In every beat
In his strong brave heart
Beats the soul of his country

Alex Gardeck
Age: 12

DO YOU KNOW?

As white as snow
As clear as day
Most people know
What I'm going to say

Today the snow is black
The day is fogged and misty
And today you don't know
Me in any way

You say you know everything
About me and everyone
You say I'm this
And I like that
But truly, I do not

If you knew everything
I'm sure that you would know
That I hate you
From your head
To your toes

You think you know my secrets
Every last one
But you don't
Know even one

You think that you're the best
That you're the one they love
But truly you're insane
'Cause you're totally wrong

You act like you run the world
Changing people's lives
You do this
You say that
Always behind a back

So now just stop
Try being me
And then maybe
You will see

You'll see the things
That you have caused
The hurt and the pain
That you love
As reality sets in
Maybe you'll see too
That people aren't like you

Annabelle Heisley
Age: 12

SKIES

Blue skies in the air.
High blue skies are over there.
Skies are here and there.

Elizabeth Hardwicke
Age: 7

GHOST

Ghost fly
t h r o u g h
the air on
Hallo-
ween
night scaring
all the little
kids and dressing up
for the site of Halloween
night. Eating   all the   candy
and   having   a   fun   time.

Kayla McDonald
Age: 9

FROST

Every morning I wake up
To check the ground
Hoping to have snow found
But as I look outside,
White fluff catches my eye.
Yet I know it's not here to stay
It's nature's frosted trick,
And will soon melt away.
So I wait until tomorrow,
But hope for later today.

Sofia B.T. Skok
Age: 14

NATURE

sky blue as water
the leaves spinning in the wind
river flowing fast

Sara Mary Bell
Age: 9

LEMON

Lemon looks like a burst of excitement
from a flaming fire,
Lemon tastes like the creamy center of lemon cake,
Lemon feels like meringue cream on my fingers,

Lemon is the wet, fuzzy tennis ball
caught in my dog Port's mouth,
Lemon is in the spotlight, always noticed,
Lemon is dressed like a movie star singing on the stage,
Lemon is a ripe tropical fruit in the rain forest,
Lemon is a tiger in a pen kept from freedom,

Lemon dreams of becoming hot pink,
Lemon remembers the sun coming up
in the morning sky with lots of fresh air,
Lemon thinks about its best friend Lime.

Teagan Moore
Age: 9

THE GIRL IN SPAIN

There once was a girl in Spain
Who loved to play in the rain
One day she slipped
And broke her hip
Now she is in serious pain

Allyson Dolci
Age: 9

SAD

Sad is ashamed
His hair, a litter of knots
His mouth drops
Like a wilted flower
His feet drag
On the ground with shame
His clothes, somber
With no color at all
Like he was going to cry
His body, stooped
Like ice cream
In the hot sun
He wanders helplessly
Lost, confused, disoriented
Sad is depressed

Thomas Segrue
Age: 12

MOONLIGHT

Moonlight shines on me
From the sky on high, night sings
Like a lovely song

Rachael Dion
Age: 9

STUFF TO DO

Blue skies, green trees.
I play with my friends
Until the day ends.
Summer nights are blue
Just what to do.

I dream.
And I eat cream.

I play every day
While the horses eat hay.
I say hooray.

I see a smile
And play awhile.
I will say good-bye
So you can try.

Melissa Kirschner

THAT CAMEO I USED TO KNOW

I looked in the full-length mirror,
And I saw something other than me.
It was a cameo of someone I used to be
A dull, boring, excuse of an oaf
Stupid, dumb, a really ugly sort.
That's when I leaned on my friends,
They helped pave the path.
That now leads to the new photograph.

I'm in a new place, a new time now.
"Please don't let it be 1944," I said aloud.
But it was not. It was beautiful, serene.
I looked around and saw all green.

The blue ocean billowed in the breeze.
This is a cameo of a place I used to be.
I realized God did this, to let me see who I am.
Then I figured out that I must go back
But I had a homesick attack.

This was the place of my birth,
I didn't want to leave!
But the space-time continuum started to heave.
I looked back once more.

A cameo of what I had done before
This was all of the things I used to be.
Then the cameo started to leave.
"Come back," I cried, "please don't flee!"
But face it, come on, this is who I used to be.
It was not a cameo of who I was, and am.

It was not a cameo I USED to know.
It was a present cameo of me.

Corrin Stines
Age: 11

CRAZY HAIR DAY

It's sticking up here and there
Crazy colors everywhere.
My hair is green and I don't care.
Do I dare to wash my hair?
So my color won't be there.
Should I hide while people stare,
I'll just pick a hat to wear.
My hair looks like it got
Attacked by a bear.
Wow many people have a fear—
Many didn't dare to stare.
Some people weren't even there.
Of course I was
But no one cared.

Haley Jacobsen

PURPLE

Purple is like the sound
of eggplant being picked.
Purple is like the smell
of purple flowers.
Purple is like the taste
of eggplant.
Purple is like the feel
of purple blankets.

Kirsten Adamski
Age: 6

ADRIANA GUTIERREZ

Adriana
Happy, nice, and sweet
Big sister of Monse and Valeria
Who loves Mexico, family, and sisters
Who feels shy to read in front of people
Who needs family, care, and chocolate
Who gives kindness
Who fears tornados, bulldogs, and snowstorms
Who'd like to see my grandma and grandpa in Mexico
Who dreams of a good family
A student at IHK
Nickname Adi

Adriana Gutierrez
Age: 9

ORANGE

Orange is like the sound
of bounce in a basketball.
Orange is like the smell
of carving a pumpkin.
Orange is like the taste
of pumpkin pie.
Orange is like the feel
of a hard pumpkin in the patch.

Rian Cudia-Rouse
Age: 8

A BEAUTIFUL CREATURE

A strong body,
A racing heart,
Misty, fiery eyes
Looking upon the world
In the wink of an eye,
It's gone
You better look fast
A powerful stare,
A mighty gait
A deep rumble comes over the Earth,
The creature is gone,
You'd better look fast

Erin Hughes
Age: 12

SILVER

Silver is like the sound
of bells ringing.
Silver is like the smell
of burning metal.
Silver is like the taste
of a new-filled cavity.
Silver is like the feel
of a very stormy day.

Sarah Coffman
Age: 7

NOW

As this goes on,
we seem to think,
that the world will soon end.
We are just too young,
to say these things,
to put this in our heads.
With all the yelling,
and crying and screaming,
you'd think that we are strong.
But inside our heads,
more than anything else,
we want this over.
Now.

Khadija Khan

ANIMALS

Mice are sometimes nice.
But they don't like ice.

Cats don't like cheese.
And can't say please.

Jessica Giraldi
Age: 8

FIREWORKS

Loud sounds from the sky
Broken pieces from the sky
Fireworks make cool things.

Chris Kerwin
Age: 10

FIREBALL

Falling from the sky
Burning rock all together
Falling on the ground

Katie Kerwin
Age: 10

MY PET MONKEY

I wish his name was Chunk
He ate a lot of junk

He had bought a huge mouse
He put it in my house

He so loves to run
He has lots of fun

Mikey Squires
Age: 8

KATIE BECKMANN

Katie
Loving, excited, kind
Sister of Julie
Who loves friends, family, and pets
Who feels nervous on tests
Who needs friends, family, and love
Who gives hugs
Who fears snakes, spiders, and sharks
Who'd like to see my grandpa
Who dreams of joining softball
A student of Miss Russ
Nickname Kaitlynn

Katie Beckmann
Age: 9

THE BLUE DOG

My dog is blue.
He likes to chew.
But then he grew.
He likes to drool.

Marty O'Brien
Age: 9

LILY FLOWER

A beautiful thing
Pretty petals with long stem
Is an awesome plant

Lilly Ross
Age: 9

DRAGON

Stomping very loud
Fire blowing fast at last
Breaking anything

Natalie Villalobos
Age: 8

A MESS FOR A DRESS

What do you think of this dress?
Well I think it is a mess.
But I have to finish the rest.
Do you think you can finish the rest?
And the dress will look the best.

Camilla Czajka
Age: 10

PLUTO EXPLODING

Exploding Pluto
In the huge solar system
Bye-bye Pluto bye

Riley Hartjes
Age: 8

SQUIGGLES

Pink and purple joy
Bursting all over the ground
Colors everywhere

McKenzie Marquez
Age: 9

MONKEY NAMED FRED

Once there was a monkey named Fred
Who had to take meds.
He took too many pills so he went mad.
His mother was very sad.
So, now Fred is dead.

Alexis Lauren Kube
Age: 9

WATERFALLS

Waterfalls, peace,
quiet, calm, relaxing.
The cold water
falling, falling
from the cliff,
way up there.
Just sitting
all the time,
in that same spot.
Steam formed
from the cool, delicate, water
against the hard, brown,
still, dead, rocks below.
Waterfalls,
always there to see
and admire.

Patrick Vitale
Age: 11

Football
fun, hard
running, kicking, tackling
makes me feel tired
Sport

Bailey C. Ristich
Age: 9

SNOWMAN

There once was an extraordinary snowman
Who went to Florida for a tan
He came back as water—
Not recognized by his daughter
Then he was driven away in a van.

Madison Hughes
Age: 10

TREES

Trees are beautiful
So beautiful with apples
So red and tasty.

Nathan Murray
Age: 9

Boys
active, crabby
yelling, fighting, running
students, learners, children, friends
talking, walking, giggling
friendly, happy
Girls

Beth Cannon
Age: 10

Spring
pretty, sunny
planting, seeding, growing
flowers, leaves, trees, winds
falling, jumping, playing
colorful, bare
Fall

Ross Brenza
Age: 9

OUR WORLD

Our world is so cool
Fifty states and even more
Blue green and pretty

Sally Dick
Age: 9

ZEBRAS

Zebras running freely
in grassy fields
looking out for hungry lions
hope they don't see me
all of our stripes are unique
so don't get us mixed up

Alexis Rouse
Age: 9

BELL

My cat Bell is very nice,
She never had a price.

She was a stray.
She was not gray.

She never bites.
She never fights.

Penelope Janicki
Age: 8

CANDY CORN

Candy corn is sweet.
It is a very good treat. You
eat it on Halloween. The
day that makes you
scream. Its beautiful
colors, look better
than others I
love candy
corn!

Britany Robinson
Age: 10

A WALK THROUGH THE PARK

I was walking there
Summer in the summer air,
Thinking to myself
about how I should just stay there,
I remembered
how I had walked this way a million times before
but didn't ever stay.
I would walk on and on
every day
without a word to say.
Now I must say
this is a wonderful way to spend the day.

Karl Rauschenberger
Age: 12

AUTUMN THROUGH THE SENSES

Autumn is the sound of
Werewolves howling in the night,
Ghosts screaming in cemeteries,
Doors creaking in haunted houses,
And wind swooshing in the distance.

Autumn smells like
Smoke from a crackling fire,
Freshly baked pumpkin pie,
Mouthwatering turkey in the oven,
And cold mist in the grass.

Autumn feels like
Gooey pumpkin guts from carving a pumpkin,
Crunched-up leaves all over my body in a leaf pile,
Wrinkled wrappers in my hands from candy,
And cozy, warm mittens on my hand.

Autumn tastes like
Freshly made apple cider,
Salty, crunchy pumpkin seeds,
Delicious, sweet candy melting in my mouth,
And yummy, crisp Halloween cookies.

Autumn looks like
Red, orange, and yellow leaves
Falling from trees gracefully,
Empty bare branches,
Smoking hot pie in the window,
And kids shivering with gloves and hats.

Jackson Prigge
Age: 9

A LOVELY THUNK

When I step onto the field,
All my problems seem to disappear.
Nothing matters to me
Except being the best I can be!
Then I step up to bat,
The pitcher adjusts her red hat,
As I watch her pitch,
It is like a graceful ballerina dancing.
The world seems to be in slow-motion
As the dirty yellow ball approaches.
I am like a tiger,
Ready to attack.
I swing! The bat and ball connect!
It makes a lovely "thunk"!
I drop my bat, and I watch my hit soar.
Two runners on base score.
The fans all go wild.
The sound is not mild.
I feel as if I've won the lottery.
I have all the fame and glory.
When I get to the bench,
I am mobbed by friends.
My coach is grinning,
As if he just met a rock star.
Then I know,
This is my best day by far!

Alexis Pezdek
Age: 12

SAFE

I descend through the wet silk dew
Cold air meets my face
Silence
Stars smile at my presence
I look out to the never-ending abyss
Black
Water
Skyline of the trees mesh
With the dark
Ominous night
Cracked wood
I sit
Warm water greets my
Tiny feet
Long strands of fuzzy seaweed
All around me now
Relaxed
On my back
I gaze up at the world
There are no words
But I can hear them
Safety
Breathing
In
And out
Heartbeat
Realization
From the water

Suddenly
A splash in the distance
Or is it close?
I'm not alone.

Nicole M. Mayerck
Age: 18

THE GREAT OUTDOORS

The outdoors is great
The squirrel runs first rate
The great horned owls meet
The deer are on the street

The little raccoon is a thief
The sun shines on the clover leaf
The coyote was relieved to see the den
The raccoon ate the hen

The screaming badgers at night
The coyotes are a sight
The deer are in a fight
The badgers were in sight

The water against the rocks gush
The cow stands in the slush
The elk hide in the brush
The outside world just a hush . . .

Nathaniel Leintz
Age: 12

MY BIRTHDAY

If every day could be my birthday,
Oh, how fun it would be.
If every day could be my birthday,
I'd shout with glee!

If every day was my birthday,
I would get presents every day.
If every day was my birthday,
I would shout "HIP, HIP, HOORAY!"

If I could have a birthday every single day,
I will be happy and gay.
If I could have a birthday every single day,
I know I would always have the best day.

If I had a birthday seven days a week,
I know I would never weep.
If I had a birthday seven days a week,
I know I could shriek for every day of the week!

If I could have a birthday
three hundred sixty-five days of a year,
I know I would have good cheer.
If I could have a birthday
three hundred sixty-five days of a year,
I would be so happy I couldn't shed a tear!

Gabriella Ramirez
Age: 12

SUMMER

Feels hot on my skin
Makes me hyper
It smells good outside
I put on suntan lotion

Zachary Eaton
Age: 8

COLOR BLUE

as skies
and oceans
and raindrops

Blue

as a present
and a car
and a poster

Blue

as a book cover
and a crayon
and a book

Blue

Blue as the Earth's oceans

Anthony Gogola
Age: 9

WILDCATS

Wildcats are winning
We're winning against the Walruses.
We won and now we're in the Super Bowl
and we're versing the Wolfs.
Now in the undefeated Wildcats verses the Wolfs.
William is our best running back.
We work our hardest to wrestle every team.

Matthew Clark
Age: 8

FRIENDS

Going to the mall together
Just hanging out at someone's house
Crazy, insane sleepovers
Painting nails or doing hair

Just hanging out at someone's house
Playing sports together
Painting nails or doing hair
Keeping secrets

Playing sports together
Eating as much candy as we can
Keeping secrets
Fun times I'll never forget

Maria Cali
Age: 11

ICE

Slipping, sliding, going fast
Gliding and blading at last
Skating fast, and skating slow
Getting where you want to go
On the ice you glide and whirl
Girls on ice like to twirl
Shining blades go very fast
'Til you find yourself in last
As the kids seem to slide
They do it with pride.

Morgan Rogers
Age: 9

SWIMMING

Swimming, swimming is such a joy.
I can even swim with a toy.

Swimming, swimming is so fun.
I like swimming in the sun.

I like swimming at the bay.
I want to swim the whole day.

Katie Beaudin
Age: 9

THE SNOWMAN

"No!" cried the man of frost,
"Just give me one last day."
But he knew from the sudden signs,
That time could not be changed.
He'd heard the cries from Red Chest;
The robin in the tree,
That spring was on its way,
And would not be delayed.
Mother Nature had told him so,
But only now did he know,
That soon it would be too late,
And there would be no snow.
As he sat there recollecting,
How short his life had been,
A drop of rain fell from the clouds,
And landed on his chin.
But when that raindrop hit him,
Like a teardrop from the sky,
He realized his time had come,
And he began to cry.
He'd have to wait another year;
Three-hundred and sixty-five days.
Until wintertime came again,
When he could then be made.
As the man sat there crying,
Getting smaller and smaller yet,
He realized in fright,
That he was extremely wet.

But this time he didn't fight it,
Because he already knew,
So he sat there and let himself melt,
Until he looked like a puddle of dew.
Although the snowman had melted,
He wasn't completely gone,
Because where his puddle had been,
Now sat his eyes, nose, and mouth on the lawn.

Morgan Paige Powers
Age: 13

GREEN

Interesting birds, lizards, frogs
Little plantlets first sprouting
Tasty green beans on the vines
Scrumptious apples on the trees

Little plantlets first sprouting
Incredible Hulk lunchboxes
Scrumptious apples on the trees
Bright green evergreens

Incredible Hulk lunchboxes
Green minivans cruising down the street
Bright green evergreens
The beautiful dark green leaves

David J. Glogowski
Age: 10

LARRY

When I have to carry
my brother named Larry,
I'd rather be trampled by oxen.
For they would give me a big knockin'.
So give him wheels!
But he'll slip on banana peels.

Adrian Gutierrez de Velasco
Age: 8

HALLOWEEN

H orrifying fear
A mazing parties
L ots of spirit
L ots of fun
O wls flying
W atching scary movies
E njoyable candy
E very right to be scared
N ighttime fright

Ryan Keane
Age: 10